WITHDRAWN

D0962021

The Conquest of the New World

Other Books in the At Issue in History Series:

The Conquest of the New World

Helen Cothran, *Book Editor*

Daniel Leone, *President*
Bonnie Szumski, *Publisher*
Scott Barbour, *Managing Editor*
Bruno Leone, *Series Editor*

AT ISSUE IN HISTORY

Greenhaven Press, Inc.
San Diego, California

No part of this book may be reproduced or used in any form or by any means, electrical, mechanical, or otherwise, including, but not limited to, photocopy, recording, or any information storage and retrieval system, without prior written permission from the publisher.

Library of Congress Cataloging-in-Publication Data

The conquest of the New World / Helen Cothran, book editor.
    p.   cm. — (At issue in history)
    Includes bibliographical references and index.
    ISBN 0-7377-1273-2 (pbk. : alk. paper) —
ISBN 0-7377-1274-0 (lib. : alk. paper)
    1. America—Discovery and exploration. 2. America—
Colonization. 3. America—Colonization—Social aspects.
4. Indians of North America—First contact with Europeans.
5. Indians, Treatment of. 6. Columbus, Christopher.
7. Colombus, Christopher—Ethics. 8. Conquerors—America—
History. 9. Explorers—America—History. I. Cothran,
Helen. II. Series.

E101 .C73 2002
970.01—dc21

                                                    2001040341

Cover photo: Hulton Getty/Archive Photos
Library of Congress, 26, 128

© 2002 by Greenhaven Press, Inc., 10911 Technology Place
San Diego, CA 92127

Printed in the U.S.A.

Every effort has been made to trace owners of copyrighted material.

Contents

Foreword

Historian Robert Weiss defines history simply as "a record and interpretation of past events." Both elements—record and interpretation—are necessary, Weiss argues.

> Names, dates, places, and events are the essence of history. But historical writing is not a compendium of facts. It consists of facts placed in a sequence to tell a connected story. A work of history is not merely a story, however. It also must analyze what happened and *why*—that is, it must interpret the past for the reader.

For example, the events of December 7, 1941, that led President Franklin D. Roosevelt to call it "a date which will live in infamy" are fairly well known and straightforward. A force of Japanese planes and submarines launched a torpedo and bombing attack on American military targets in Pearl Harbor, Hawaii. The surprise assault sank five battleships, disabled or sank fourteen additional ships, and left almost twenty-four hundred American soldiers and sailors dead. On the following day, the United States formally entered World War II when Congress declared war on Japan.

These facts and consequences were almost immediately communicated to the American people who heard reports about Pearl Harbor and President Roosevelt's response on the radio. All realized that this was an important and pivotal event in American and world history. Yet the news from Pearl Harbor raised many unanswered questions. Why did Japan decide to launch such an offensive? Why were the attackers so successful in catching America by surprise? What did the attack reveal about the two nations, their people, and their leadership? What were its causes, and what were its effects? Political leaders, academic historians, and students look to learn the basic facts of historical events and to read the intepretations of these events by many different sources, both primary and secondary, in order to develop a more complete picture of the event in a historical context.

In the case of Pearl Harbor, several important questions surrounding the event remain in dispute, most notably the role of President Roosevelt. Some historians have blamed his policies for deliberately provoking Japan to attack in order to propel America into World War II; a few have gone so far as to accuse him of knowing of the impending attack but not informing others. Other historians, examining the same event, have exonerated the president of such charges, arguing that the historical evidence does not support such a theory.

The Greenhaven At Issue in History series recognizes that many important historical events have been interpreted differently and in some cases remain shrouded in controversy. Each volume features a collection of articles that focus on a topic that has sparked controversy among eyewitnesses, contemporary observers, and historians. An introductory essay sets the stage for each topic by presenting background and context. Several chapters then examine different facets of the subject at hand with readings chosen for their diversity of opinion. Each selection is preceded by a summary of the author's main points and conclusions. A bibliography is included for those students interested in pursuing further research. An annotated table of contents and thorough index help readers to quickly locate material of interest. Taken together, the contents of each of the volumes in the Greenhaven At Issue in History series will help students become more discriminating and thoughtful readers of history.

Introduction

Many historians agree that Christopher Columbus pursued three goals that influenced the conquistadors who followed him: God, gold, and glory. Believing that the natives lacked religion, Columbus wanted to bring Christianity to the Indians in his newfound Eden. This is made clear in a November 11, 1492, entry in his log addressed to Ferdinand V and Isabella I, the Spanish monarchs who financed his journey: "I see and know that these people have no religion whatever, nor are they idolaters . . . Your Highnesses must resolve to make them Christians. I believe that if this effort commences, in a short time a multitude of peoples will be converted to our Holy Faith."

His search for gold is also revealed in his ship's log. Rumors of gold repeatedly lured him on to explore yet another island. With gold, Columbus could fulfill his promise of untold riches to the crown, become wealthy himself, and provide a measure of prestige to his family.

Glory, too, consumed him. The agreement between Columbus and the monarchs, known as the Capitulations of Santa Fe and signed on April 17, 1492, established this motive. Throughout the document, Columbus is referred to as Don Cristobal Colón. It seems obvious that the status of nobleman was a part of or preceded the agreement. In addition, the monarchs promised him the rank of admiral for life, the title to be passed on in perpetuity to his heirs. He was to be viceroy and governor general of all islands and mainland he might discover. Finally, of all wealth "whether pearls, precious stones, gold, silver, spices . . . which may be bought, bartered, discovered, acquired and obtained," Ferdinand and Isabella agreed to grant Columbus "the tenth part of the whole," after expenses, reserving the other nine parts for themselves.

John Noble Wilford, author of *The Mysterious History of Columbus*, analyzes the significance of this agreement:

> Beyond its authorization of royal support, the document's significance lies in the insight it affords into

Columbus's paramount interests and intentions. He had struck a business deal. He can be seen here as a grasping merchant with an eye to securing a monopoly on the riches he expected to find in lands he intended to exploit, much as he had witnessed the Portuguese doing on the African coast. An exploitative attitude toward America and native Americans was thus fixed at the outset. And this attitude was normal for the times. Exploration, more often than not, is motivated not by scientific and geographic curiosity but by the quest for wealth and power; it would be anachronistic to believe it otherwise in a society two centuries before the Scientific Revolution.

The Spanish conquistadors who followed Columbus shared his dream. Like Columbus, Cortés and Pizarro, Balboa and de Soto, Alvarado and Zarate sailed to the New World in search of gold, glory, and converts to Christianity. Many of these men were attempting to escape the grinding poverty in Spain. Out of this struggle against poverty came one of the most enduring images of the New World—a land of opportunity, a place of new beginnings.

The Spanish conquistadors, in their contacts with the native peoples of the Americas, established patterns of behavior and demonstrated attitudes that other colonial powers would later display. One of the attitudes that the Spaniards held was an absolute conviction that Christianity was the one, true religion. The Spaniards, flush from their victory against the Moors who had occupied Spain for centuries, were militant Christians who had warred with the infidel and were now determined to make new converts in the Americas. This determination was reinforced when native religious practices horrified the conquistadors. Soldiers with Cortés in the conquest of New Spain were repulsed and terrified by the ritual sacrifice and cannibalism practiced by the Aztecs. When Cortés's efforts to sway the natives from these practices failed, the Spaniards became convinced that they needed to eradicate them by military means.

Despite their revulsion at some of the native religious practices, many of the conquistadors were awed by the size and sophistication of the cities in Mexico and Peru. Spanish soldiers, most from the Spanish provinces, had never seen cities such as Tenochtitlan (the Aztec capital on the site of present-day Mexico City), which easily rivaled the mini-metropolises of Paris or London. Bernal Díaz, a soldier in Cortés's army, describes Mexico's capital city as if he's fallen into a magical kingdom. An intricate system of lakes and causeways linked elegant palaces and imposing temples. Stalls of skilled craftsmen—jewelers and goldsmiths and featherworkers—dotted the thoroughfares. Zoos, aviaries, and gardens provided recreation for the nobles. Throughout the city, entertainers—stiltwalkers, clowns, and dancers—performed to the amusement of all onlookers. Even the market was grander than any other the European world had to offer. Díaz states: "Some of our soldiers who had been in . . . Constantinople, in Rome, and all over Italy, said that they had never seen a market so well laid out, so large, so orderly, and so full of people." In the face of such opulence and sophistication, it must have been difficult for simple men from Spanish provinces to maintain their previously unquestioned sense of superiority to the natives.

A similar discrepancy may be seen in the attitudes of the missionaries who accompanied the conquest. While it is true that some priests zealously consigned precious native documents and artifacts to the flames as works of the Devil, others, like Torbio Motolinia, carefully described and documented native culture. And while some priests overlooked the cruel treatment of the Indians by soldiers and colonists, others, like Bartolomé de las Casas, became strong and outspoken advocates of humane treatment of the Indians.

Yet despite occasional displays of enlightenment, the Spaniards quickly worked to establish military dominance. Although their military superiority probably could not have been achieved without the unintentional ally of communicable disease, especially smallpox, Spanish military technology—ships that used sails as well as oars, arquebuses, cannons, metal armor and swords—was formidable. Effective, too, were their four-footed companions, the mastiffs and the horses.

It was partly with the help of the horse and partly due to Spanish shipbuilding skills that Cortés and his compatriots conquered the Aztecs. The conquest of Tenochtitlan was well documented by Cortés himself. In two dispatches, which he sent to the Spanish monarchs, he describes the opulence of Tenochtitlan and the ritual human sacrifice and cannibalism that occurred in the city's temples. Both the booty to be taken and the barbarism to be quashed provided strong incentives for the Spanish to take over the city. When Cortés and his men first arrived outside Tenochtitlan, the Aztec's leader, Montezuma, welcomed them in and treated them hospitably. But the conquistadors quickly discovered that while they remained within the city, they were trapped. Tenochtitlan was surrounded by a series of causeways and was only accessible by bridges that could be removed by the Aztecs at any time. Fearing for their lives, the Spanish took Montezuma captor and eventually attempted to flee the city. However, the Aztecs attacked them and managed to kill many horses and men before the retreat was accomplished. Vowing revenge, Cortés devised a plan to retake the city. He ordered brigantines to be built by which they could sail over the causeways to the city without relying on the removable bridges. This second effort was successful with Cortés taking control of the entire Aztec empire.

Other conquistadors who had a prominent role in the conquest of the New World include Francisco Pizzaro, Hernando de Soto, Vasco Nuñez de Balboa, Ferdinand Magellan, and Panfilo de Narváez. Pizzaro is famous for conquering the Inca Empire in Peru, and for founding the city of Lima. De Soto, who also helped conquer Peru, led an expedition into North America where he explored Mississippi, Florida, and Georgia. Balboa was the first white person to cross the Isthmus of Panama and see the Pacific Ocean, while Magellan was the first man to circumnavigate the world. Lastly, Narváez led an ill-fated expedition to Florida, which resulted in only four survivors returning to New Spain.

In addition to military conquest, the Spanish conquistadors began to forcibly seize land from the Indians to be used for colonization. In both New Spain and North America, colonists settled on land that was being used by the Indians for hunting, gathering, and cultivating crops. The Indian response to those uninvited and unwelcomed visitors was active resistance. Bloody wars between colonist and aboriginal became common until the Indians were eventually forced off their land and made to settle in less hospitable locales or on reservations.

The colonists not only took land from the natives to live on, but they began to exploit the land in ways foreign to the Indians. For example, while most Indian tribes had a reverent regard for nature and lived in harmony with it, the Spaniards sought to extract nature's riches: gold in Mexico, pearls at the mouth of the Orinoco River, and silver at Potosi. The Indians found longing for riches strange. The Aztecs observed the Spanish response to gifts of gold:

> And when they were given these presents, the Spaniards burst into smiles; their eyes shone with pleasure; they were delighted by them. They picked up the gold and fingered it like monkeys; they seemed to be transported by joy, as if their hearts were illumined and made new. The truth is that they longed and lusted for gold. Their bodies swelled with greed, and their hunger was ravenous; they hungered like pigs for that gold.

When exploitation of the land's mineral resources became less profitable, plantations were established, especially in the Caribbean and in Brazil. The "white gold," sugar, became an additional source of wealth. To the European, land was to be worked and made to yield a profit. The conquistadors also brought back from the New World corn and the potato, two important staples which significantly changed the diets of the peoples of Europe.

Historian Alfred W. Crosby Jr. calls the process of exchanges between the New World and the Old World the "Columbian exchange," named after Christopher Columbus, the man who inaugurated them. In 1992, the Smithsonian Institution created an exhibit on the Columbian exchange which it named "Seeds of Change." It selected five catalysts, or "seeds," which had far-reaching consequences for both the Old and New Worlds: disease, the horse, corn, the potato, and sugar.

Diseases such as smallpox were unintentionally transported to the New World by the conquistadors and their crews. Once unleashed, these diseases quickly decimated the native population, which had no resistance to European diseases. Smallpox was responsible for up to a 90 percent of deaths within the native population during the first century after contact. Disease became the most powerful and unexpected ally of the conquerors of Mexico. The horse also became a catalyst for change in Indian culture. It gave the Plains Indians of North America greater mobility, transforming hunting practices and bringing tribes into greater contact with one another. Food exchanges between the Old and New World also effected great change. While the conquistadors at first disapproved of the Indians' crops of corn and potatoes, the prospect of starvation brought about a quick change of heart. These staples provided a greater number of calories per acre than did the Old World wheat, barley, rice and rye, and were therefore more economical to grow. In contrast, sugar was a mixed blessing. When the conquistadors first decided to plant sugar crops in the New World, they found that processing sugar was labor-intensive and required a huge native labor pool. With Indian slaves dying in such large numbers from disease and harsh treatment, the colonists began to import indentured servants and slaves from Africa to work in the sugar industry. In addition, the sugar industry resulted in environmental destruction through deforestation.

Although the Columbian exchange left a legacy of far-reaching, worldwide changes, such exchanges were not on the minds of the conquistadors when they conquered and eventually colonized the New World. On the contrary, the conquistadors' astonishing persistence in enduring the hardships and dangers of exploration and conquest was motivated by the trinity of God, gold, and glory. One of the ironies for many of the conquistadors was that they died without wealth or prestige. Bernal Díaz died a poor man, aware that he had been treated unfairly by his leaders. Hernando de Soto died of a fever, and his body was thrown into the Mississippi River to prevent capture by the Indians. Panfilo de Narváez drowned. Pedro de Alvarado, who saw active duty in Mexico and Guatemala, was crushed to death by a horse. Pedro de Valdivia, conqueror of Chile, was eaten by cannibals. One can hope that in these travails, and lacking gold and glory, the conquistadors at least had their God.

Chapter 1

Christopher Columbus

1

Columbus Was a Hero

Samuel Eliot Morison

Adm. Samuel Eliot Morison won a Pulitzer prize for *Admiral of the Ocean Sea: A Life of Christopher Columbus.* An avid sailor, Morison undertook an expedition in 1939 to sail a 147-foot yacht, *Capitania*, to the New World, following Columbus's route as closely as possible. His explanation: "You cannot write a story out of these fifteenth and sixteenth century narratives that means anything to a modern reader, merely by studying them in a library with the aid of maps." Thus, written by an author immersed in the practical difficulties of sailing the Atlantic, *Admiral of the Ocean Sea* has been, since its publication in 1942, the definitive biography against which other Columbus scholars are measured. Morison's other books include *The Two Ocean War: A Short History of the United States Navy in the Second World War* and *John Paul Jones: A Sailor's Biography.* Morison was professor emeritus of history at Harvard University. His fascination with, and admiration of, Columbus was profound. While his biography does not ignore Columbus's flaws, it tends to demonstrate his epic dimensions.

Let us pause and find out if we can what manner of man was this Columbus at the dangerous age of thirty— dangerous that is in youthful ambition, to ideals and visions, the age that makes others settle down, drains the fire from ardent youth, turns men into tabby cats content to sit by the fire. Hear what was said about Columbus by men who knew him, and whose lives crossed his.

No description of Columbus at this precise period exists; we have to work back from what people said of him af-

From *Admiral of the Ocean Sea*, by Samuel Eliot Morison. Copyright © 1942 by Samuel Eliot Morison; renewed © 1970 by Samuel Eliot Morison. Reprinted by permission of Little, Brown, and Company (Inc.).

ter the great achievement. Oviedo, who witnessed the Admiral's triumphant entry into Barcelona in 1493, says this of him in a work that was printed forty years later: "A man of honest parents and life, of good stature and appearance, taller than the average and strongly limbed: the eyes lively and other parts of the face of good proportion, the hair very red, and the face somewhat ruddy and freckled; fair in speech, tactful and of a great creative talent; a nice Latinist and most learned cosmographer; gracious when he wished to be, irascible when annoyed."

Columbus Described by His Son

Ferdinand Columbus, who was with his father constantly between the ages of twelve and eighteen, has this description in his biography:

The Admiral was a well built man of more than medium stature, long visaged with cheeks somewhat high, but neither fat nor thin. He had an aquiline nose and his eyes were light in color; his complexion too was light, but kindling to a vivid red. In youth his hair was blond, but when he came to his thirtieth year it all turned white. In eating and drinking and the adornment of his person he was always continent and modest. Among strangers his conversation was affable, and with members of his household very pleasant, but with a modest and pleasing dignity. In matters of religion he was so strict that for fasting and saying all the canonical offices he might have been taken for a member of a religious order. And he was so great an enemy to cursing and swearing, that I swear I never heard him utter any other oath than "by San Fernando!" and when he was most angry with anyone, his reprimand was to say, "May God take you!" for doing or saying that. And when he had to write anything, he would not try the pen without first writing these words, *Jesus cum Maria sit nobis in via* [Jesus and Mary be with us on the way], and in such fair letters that he might have gained his bread by them alone.

Las Casas' View of Columbus

Las Casas, who saw the Admiral in Hispaniola in 1500, and whose father and uncle had been shipmates and colonists under him, amplifies Ferdinand's description in the *Historia de las Indias:*

As regards his exterior person and bodily disposition, he was more than middling tall; face long and giving an air of authority; aquiline nose, blue eyes, complexion light and tending to bright red; beard and hair red when young but very soon turned gray from his labors; he was affable and cheerful in speaking, . . . eloquent and boastful in his negotiations; he was serious in moderation, affable with strangers, and with members of his household gentle and pleasant, with modest gravity and discreet conversation; and so could easily incite those who saw him to love him. In fine, he was most impressive in his port and countenance, a person of great state and authority and worthy of all reverence. He was sober and moderate in eating, drinking, clothing and footwear; it was commonly said that he spoke cheerfully in familiar conversation, or with indignation when he gave reproof or was angry with somebody: "May God take you, don't you agree to this and that?" or "Why have you done this and that?" In matters of the Christian religion, without doubt he was a Catholic and of great devotion; for in everything he did and said or sought to begin, he always interposed "In the name of the Holy Trinity I will do this," or "launch this" or "this will come to pass." In whatever letter or other thing he wrote, he put at the head "Jesus and Mary be with us on the way.". . .

In matters of religion [Columbus] was so strict that for fasting and saying all the canonical offices he might have been taken for a member of a religious order.

He observed the fasts of the Church most faithfully, confessed and made communion often, read the canonical offices like a churchman or member of a religious order, hated blasphemy and profane swearing, was most devoted to Our Lady and to the seraphic father St. Francis; seemed very grateful to God for benefits received from the divine hand, wherefore, as in the proverb, he hourly admitted that God had conferred upon him great mercies, as upon David. When gold or precious things were brought to him, he entered his cabin, knelt down, summoned the bystanders, and said, "Let us give thanks to Our Lord that he has thought us worthy to discover so many good things." He was extraordinarily zealous for the divine service; he desired and was eager for the conversion of these people [the Indians], and that in every region the faith of Jesus Christ be planted and enhanced. . . .

He was a gentleman of great force of spirit, of lofty thoughts, naturally inclined (from what one may gather of his life, deeds, writings and conversation) to undertake worthy deeds and signal enterprises; patient and long-suffering (as later shall appear), and a forgiver of injuries, and wished nothing more than that those who offended against him should recognize their errors, and that the delinquents be reconciled with him; most constant and endowed with forbearance in the hardships and adversities which were always occurring and which were incredible and infinite; ever holding great confidence in divine providence. And verily, from what I have heard from him and from my own father, who was with him when he returned to colonize Hispaniola in 1493, and from others who accompanied and served him, he held and always kept on terms of intimate fidelity and devotion to the Sovereigns.

Judging Columbus

So Columbus appeared to those who knew him, and who took pains to study his character and set it down a few years after his death. The reader will have ample opportunity to judge the Discoverer's character for himself. Physical courage, which the early historians took for granted, he will find in plenty; and untiring persistence and unbreakable will. Certain defects will appear, especially lack of due appreciation for the labors of his subordinates; unwillingness to admit his shortcomings as a colonizer; a tendency to complain and be sorry for himself whenever the Sovereigns, owing to these shortcomings, withdrew some measure of their trust in him. These were the defects of the qualities that made him a great historical figure. For he was not, like a Washington, a Cromwell or a Bolivar, an instrument chosen by multitudes to express their wills and lead a cause; Columbus was a Man with a Mission, and such men are apt to be unreasonable and even disagreeable to those who cannot see the mission. There was no psalm-singing New Model, no Spirit of '76, no Army of Liberation with drums and trumpets behind Columbus. He was Man alone with God against human stupidity and depravity, against greedy conquistadors, cowardly seamen, even against nature and the sea.

Always with God, though; in that his biographers were right; for God is with men who for a good cause put their trust in Him. Men may doubt this, but there can be no doubt that the faith of Columbus was genuine and sincere, and that his frequent communion with forces unseen was a vital element in his achievement. It gave him confidence in his destiny, assurance that his performance would be equal to the promise of his name. This conviction that God destined him to be an instrument for spreading the faith was far more potent than the desire to win glory, wealth and worldly honors, to which he was certainly far from indifferent. . . .

[Columbus] was a gentleman of great force of spirit, of lofty thoughts, naturally inclined . . . to undertake worthy deeds and signal enterprises; patient and long-suffering.

America would eventually have been discovered if the Great Enterprise of Columbus had been rejected; yet who can predict what would have been the outcome? The voyage that took him to "The Indies" and home was no blind chance, but the creation of his own brain and soul, long studied, carefully planned, repeatedly urged on indifferent princes, and carried through by virtue of his courage, sea-knowledge and indomitable will. No later voyage could ever have such spectacular results, and Columbus's fame would have been secure had he retired from the sea in 1493. Yet a lofty ambition to explore further, to organize the territories won for Castile, and to complete the circuit of the globe, sent him thrice more to America. These voyages, even more than the first, proved him to be the greatest navigator of his age, and enabled him to train the captains and pilots who were to display the banners of Spain off every American cape and island between Fifty North and Fifty South. The ease with which he dissipated the unknown terrors of the Ocean, the skill with which he found his way out and home, again and again, led thousands of men from every Western European nation into maritime adventure and exploration. And if Columbus was a failure as a colonial administrator, it was partly because his conception of a colony transcended the desire of his followers to impart, and the capacity of natives to receive, the institutions and culture of Renaissance Europe.

Columbus had a proud, passionate and sensitive nature that suffered deeply from the contempt to which he was early subjected, and the envy, disloyalty, ingratitude and injustice which he met as a discoverer. He wrote so freely out of the abundance of his complaint, as to give the impression that his life was more full of woe than of weal. That impression is false. As with other mariners, a month at sea healed the wounds of a year ashore, and a fair wind blew away the memory of foul weather. Command of a tall and gallant ship speeding over blue water before a fresh trade wind, shaping her course for some new and marvelous land where gold is abundant and the women are kind, is a mariner's dream of the good life. Columbus had a Hellenic sense of wonder at the new and strange, combined with an artist's appreciation of natural beauty; and his voyages to this strange new world brought him to some of the most gorgeous coastlines on the earth's surface. Moreover, Columbus had a deep conviction of the immanence, the sovereignty and the infinite wisdom of God, which transcended all his suffering, and enhanced all his triumphs. Waste no pity on the Admiral of the Ocean Sea! He enjoyed long stretches of pure delight such as only a seaman may know, and moments of high, proud exultation that only a discoverer can experience.

One only wishes that the Admiral might have been afforded the sense of fulfillment that would have come from foreseeing all that flowed from his discoveries; that would have turned all the sorrows of his last years to joy. The whole history of the Americas stems from the Four Voyages of Columbus; and as the Greek city-states looked back to the deathless gods as their founders, so today a score of independent nations and dominions unite in homage to Christopher the stout-hearted son of Genoa, who carried Christian civilization across the Ocean Sea.

2

Columbus Was a Pitiable Man

Justin Winsor

Justin Winsor was one of the first historians to write that Columbus was a flawed person, not an epic hero. In his biography, *Christopher Columbus and How He Received and Imparted the Spirit of Discovery*, Winsor took a far more critical look at Columbus than was customary at the time. Although Winsor acknowledges Columbus's courage and accepts the importance of his discovery, he attacks the explorer's behavior and morality for such actions as usurping the lookout's credit for sighting land and thus stealing his legitimate reward. Winsor himself became the center of a firestorm of criticism from those who preferred the heroic Columbus. Typical of such critics was Chauncey DePew, president of the New York Central Railroad, speaking at Columbus Day ceremonies in 1892: "If there is anything which I detest more than another, it is that spirit of critical historical inquiry which doubts everything; that modern spirit which destroys all the illusions and all the heroes which have been the inspiration of patriotism through all the centuries."

No man craves more than Columbus to be judged with all the palliations demanded of a difference of his own age and ours. No child of any age ever did less to improve his contemporaries, and few ever did more to prepare the way for such improvements. The age created him and the age left him. There is no more conspicuous example in history of a man showing the path and losing it.

From *Christopher Columbus and How He Received and Imparted the Spirit of Discovery*, by Justin Winsor (Boston: Houghton Mifflin, 1892).

It is by no means sure, with all our boast of benevolent progress, that atrocities not much short of those which we ascribe to Columbus and his compeers may not at any time disgrace the coming as they have blackened the past years of the nineteenth century. This fact gives us the right to judge the infirmities of man in any age from the high vantage-ground of the best emotions of all the centuries. In the application of such perennial justice Columbus must inevitably suffer. The degradation of the times ceases to be an excuse when the man to be judged stands on the pinnacle of the ages. The biographer cannot forget, indeed, that Columbus is a portrait set in the surroundings of his times; but it is equally his duty at the same time to judge the paths which he trod by the scale of an eternal nobleness.

Columbus Did Not Change World History

The very domination of this man in the history of two hemispheres warrants us in estimating him by an austere sense of occasions lost and of opportunities embraced. The really great man is superior to his age, and anticipates its future; not as a sudden apparition, but as the embodiment of a long growth of ideas of which he is the inheritor and the capable exemplar. . . . It is extremely doubtful if any instance can be found of a great idea changing the world's history, which has been created by any single man. None such was created by Columbus. There are always forerunners whose agency is postponed because the times are not propitious. A masterful thought has often a long pedigree, starting from a remote antiquity, but it will be dormant till it is environed by the circumstances suited to fructify it. This was just the destiny of the intuition which began with Aristotle and came down to Columbus. To make his first voyage partook of foolhardiness, as many a looker-on reasonably declared. It was none the less foolhardy when it was done. If he had reached the opulent and powerful kings of the Orient, his little cockboats and their brave souls might have fared hard for their intrusion. His blunder in geography very likely saved him from annihilation.

The character of Columbus has been variously drawn, almost always with a violent projection of the limner's own personality. We find [William H.] Prescott contending that "whatever the defects of Columbus's mental constitution, the finger of the historian will find it difficult to point to a single blemish in his moral character." It is certainly difficult to point to a more flagrant disregard of truth than when we find Prescott further saying, "Whether we contemplate his character in its public or private relations, in all its features it wears the same noble aspects. It was in perfect harmony with the grandeur of his plans, and with results more stupendous than those which Heaven has permitted any other mortal to achieve." It is very striking to find Prescott, after thus speaking of his private as well as public character, and forgetting the remorse of Columbus for the social wrongs he had committed, append in a footnote to this very passage a reference to his "illegitimate" son. It seems to mark an obdurate purpose to disguise the truth. This is also nowhere more patent than in the palliating hero-worship of [Washington] Irving, with his constant effort to save a world's exemplar for the world's admiration, and more for the world's sake than for Columbus's. . . . The Admiral was certainly not destitute of keen observation of nature, but unfortunately this quality was not infrequently prostituted to ignoble purposes. . . . It would have been better for the fame of Columbus if he had kept this scientific survey in its purity. It was simply, for instance, a vitiated desire to astound that made him mingle theological and physical theories about the land of Paradise. Such jugglery was promptly weighed in Spain and Italy by Peter Martyr and others as the wild, disjointed effusions of an overwrought mind, and "the reflex of a false erudition," as [Alexander von] Humboldt expresses it. It was palpably by another effort, of a like kind, that he seized upon the views of the fathers of the Church that the earthly Paradise lay in the extreme Orient, and he was quite as audacious when he exacted the oath on the Cuban coast, to make it appear by it that he had really reached the outermost parts of Asia.

Humboldt seeks to explain this errant habit by calling it "the sudden movement of his ardent and passionate soul; the disarrangement of ideas which were the effect of an incoherent method and of the extreme rapidity of his reading; while all was increased by his misfortunes and religious mysticism." Such an explanation hardly relieves the subject of it from blunter imputations. This urgency for some responsive wonderment at every experience appears constantly in the journal of Columbus's first voyage, as, for instance, when he makes every harbor exceed in beauty the last he had seen. This was the commonplace exaggeration which in our day is confined to the calls of speculating land companies. The fact was that Humboldt transferred to his hero something of the superlative love of nature that he himself had experienced in the same regions; but there was all the difference between him and Columbus that there is between a genuine love of nature and a commercial use of it. Whenever Columbus could divert his mind from a purpose to make the Indies a paying investment, we find some signs of an insight that shows either observation of his own or the garnering of it from others, as, for example, when he remarks on the decrease of rain in the Canaries and the Azores which followed upon the felling of trees, and when he conjectures that the elongated shape of the islands of the Antilles on the lines of the parallels was due to the strength of the equatorial current. . . .

Columbus Was Erratic Throughout His Life

The mental hallucinations of Columbus, so patent in his last years, were not beyond recognition at a much earlier age, and those who would get the true import of his character must trace these sorrowful manifestations to their beginnings, and distinguish accurately between Columbus when his purpose was lofty and unselfish and himself again when he became mercenary and erratic. . . .

That Columbus was a devout Catholic, according to the Catholicism of his epoch, does not admit of question, but when tried by any test that finds the perennial in holy acts, Columbus fails to bear the examination. He had nothing of the generous and noble spirit of a conjoint lover of man and of God, as the higher spirits of all times have developed it. There was no all-loving Deity in his conception. His Lord was one in whose name it was convenient to practice enormities. He shared this subterfuge with Isabella and the rest. We need to think on what Las Casas could be among his contemporaries, if we hesitate to apply the conceptions of an everlasting humanity.

The mines which Columbus went to seek were hard to find. The people he went to save to Christ were easy to exterminate. He mourned bitterly that his own efforts were ill requited. He had no pity for the misery of others, except they be his dependents and co-sharers of his purposes. He found a policy worth commemorating in slitting the noses and tearing off the ears of a naked heathen. He vindicates his excess by impressing upon the world that a man setting out to conquer the Indies must not be judged by the amenities of life which belong to a quiet rule in established countries. Yet, with a chance to establish a humane life among peoples ready to be moulded to good purposes, he sought from the very first to organize among them the inherited evils of "established countries." He talked a great deal about making converts of the poor souls, while the very first sight which he had of them prompted him to consign them to the slave-mart, just as if the first step to Christianize was the step which unmans.

Columbus's Cruelties to the Natives

The first vicar apostolic sent to teach the faith in Santo Domingo returned to Spain, no longer able to remain, powerless, in sight of the cruelties practiced by Columbus. Isabella prevented the selling of the natives as slaves in Spain, when Columbus had dispatched thither five shiploads. Las Casas tells us that in 1494–96 Columbus

Christopher Columbus

was generally hated in Española for his odiousness and injustice, and that the Admiral's policy with the natives killed a third of them in those two years. The Franciscans, when they arrived at the island, found the colonists exuberant that they had been relieved of the rule which Columbus had instituted; and the Benedictines and Dominicans added their testimony to the same effect.

The very first words, as has been said, that he used, in conveying to expectant Europe the wonders of his discovery, suggested a scheme of enslaving the strange people. He had already made the voyage that of a kidnapper, by entrapping nine of the unsuspecting natives.

On his second voyage he sent home a vessel-load of slaves, on the pretense of converting them, but his sovereigns intimated to him that it would cost less to convert them in their own homes. Then he thought of the righteous alternative of sending some to Spain to be sold to buy provisions to support those who would convert others in their homes. The monarchs were perhaps dazed at this sophistry; and Columbus again sent home four vessels laden with reeking cargoes of flesh. When he returned to Spain, in 1496, to circumvent his enemies, he once more sought in his turn, and by his reasoning, to cheat the devil of heathen souls by sending other cargoes. At last the line was drawn. It was not to save their souls, but to punish them for daring to war against the Spaniards, that they should be made to endure such horrors.

Columbus was generally hated in Española for his odiousness and injustice, and . . . [his] policy with the natives killed a third of them in . . . two years.

It is to Columbus, also, that we trace the beginning of that monstrous guilt which Spanish law sanctioned under the name of *repartimientos,* and by which to every colonist, and even to the vilest, absolute power was given over as many natives as his means and rank entitled him to hold. Las Casas tells us that Ferdinand could hardly have had a conception of the enormities of the system. If so, it was because he winked out of sight the testimony of observers, while he listened to the tales prompted of greed, rapine, and cruelty. The value of the system to force heathen out of hell, and at the same time to replenish his treasury, was the side of it presented to Ferdinand's mind by such as had access to his person. In 1501, we find the Dominicans entering their protest, and by this Ferdinand was moved to take the counsel of men learned in the law and in what passed in those days for Christian ethics. This court of appeal approved these necessary efforts, as was claimed, to increase those who were new to the faith, and to reward those who supported it.

Evil and Cupidity

Peter Martyr expressed the comforting sentiments of the age: "National right and that of the Church concede personal liberty to man. State policy, however, demurs. Custom repels the idea. Long experience shows that slavery is necessary to prevent those returning to their idolatry and error whom the Church has once gained." All professed servants of the Church, with a few exceptions like Las Casas, ranged themselves with Columbus on the side of such specious thoughts; and Las Casas, in recognizing this fact, asks what we could expect of an old sailor and fighter like Columbus, when the wisest and most respectable of the priesthood backed him in his views. It was indeed the misery of Columbus to miss the opportunity of being wiser than his fellows, the occasion always sought by a commanding spirit, and it was offered to him almost as to no other.

There was no restraining the evil. The cupidity of the colonists overcame all obstacles. The Queen was beguiled into giving equivocal instructions to Ovando, who succeeded to Bobadilla, and out of them by interpretation grew an increase of the monstrous evil. In 1503, every atrocity had reached a legal recognition. Labor was forced; the slaves were carried whither the colonists willed; and for eight months at least in every year, families were at pleasure disrupted without mercy. One feels some satisfaction in seeing Columbus himself at last, in a letter to Diego, December 1, 1504, shudder at the atrocities of Ovando. When one sees the utter annihilation of the whole race of the Antilles, a thing clearly assured at the date of the death of Columbus, one wishes that that dismal death-bed in Valladolid could have had its gloom illumined by a consciousness that the hand which lifted the banner of Spain and of Christ at San Salvador had done something to stay the misery which cupidity and perverted piety had put in course. When a man seeks to find and parades reasons for committing a crime, it is to stifle his conscience. Columbus passed years in doing it. . . .

Columbus as Mercenary

The downfall of Columbus began when he wrested from the reluctant monarchs what he called his privileges, and when he insisted upon riches as the accompaniment of such state and consequence as those privileges might entail. The terms were granted, so far as the King was concerned, simply to put a stop to importunities, for he never anticipated being called upon to confirm them. The insistency of Columbus in this respect is in strange contrast to the satisfaction which the captains of Prince Henry, Da Gama and the rest, were content to find in the unpolluted triumphs of science. The mercenary Columbus . . . was wont to say that gold gave the soul its flight to paradise. Perhaps he referred to the masses which could be bought, or to the alms which could propitiate Heaven. He might better have remembered the words of warning given to Baruch: "Seekest thou great things for thyself? Seek them not. For, saith the Lord, thy life will I give unto them for a prey in all places whither thou goest." And a prey in all places he became. . . .

No man ever evinced less capacity for ruling a colony.

If Columbus had found riches in the New World as easily as he anticipated, it is possible that such affluence would have moulded his character in other ways for good or for evil. He soon found himself confronting a difficult task, to satisfy with insufficient means a craving which his exaggerations had established. This led him to spare no device, at whatever sacrifice of the natives, to produce the coveted gold, and it was an ingenious mockery that induced him to deck his captives with golden chains and parade them through the Spanish towns. . . .

Ambition Defiled Purpose

When we view the character of Columbus in its influence upon the minds of men, we find some strange anomalies. Before his passion was tainted with the ambition of wealth and its consequence, and while he was urging the acceptance of his views for their own sake, it is very evident that he impressed others in a way that never happened after he had secured his privileges. It is after this turning-point of his life that we begin to see his falsities and indiscretions, or at least to find record of them. The incident of the moving light in the night before his first landfall is a striking instance of his daring disregard of all the qualities that help a commander in his dominance over his men. It needs little discrimination to discern the utter deceitfulness of that pretense. A noble desire to win the loftiest honors of the discovery did not satisfy a mean, insatiable greed. He blunted every sentiment of generosity when he deprived a poor sailor of his pecuniary reward. That there was no actual light to be seen is apparent from the distance that the discoverers sailed before they saw land, since if the light had been ahead they would not have gone on, and if it had been abeam they would not have left it. The evidence is that of himself and a thrall and he kept it secret at the time. The author of the *Historie* sees the difficulty, and attempts to vaporize the whole story by saying that the light was spiritual, and not physical. Navarete passes it by as a thing necessary, for the fame of Columbus, to be ignored.

His degradation began when he debased a noble purpose to the level of mercenary claims.

A second instance of Columbus's luckless impotence, at a time when an honorable man would have relied upon his character, was the attempt to make it appear that he had reached the coast of Asia by imposing an oath on his men to that effect, in penalty of having their tongues wrenched out if they recanted. One can hardly conceive a more debasing exercise of power.

His insistence upon territorial power was the serious mistake of his life. He thought, in making an agreement with his sovereigns to become a viceroy, that he was securing an honor; he was in truth pledging his happiness and beggaring his life. He sought to attain that which the fates had unfitted him for, and the Spanish monarchs, in an evil day, which was in due time their regret, submitted to his hallucinated dictation. No man ever evinced less capacity for ruling a colony.

The most sorrowful of all the phases of Columbus's character is that hapless collapse, when he abandoned all faith in the natural world, and his premonitions of it, and threw himself headlong into the vortex of what he called inspiration.

Everything in his scientific argument had been logical. It produced the reliance which comes of wisdom. It was a manly show of an incisive reason. If he had rested here his claims for honor, he would have ranked with the great seers of the universe, with Copernicus and the rest. His successful suit with the Spanish sovereigns turned his head, and his degradation began when he debased a noble purpose to the level of mercenary claims. He relied, during his first voyage, more on chicanery in controlling his crew than upon the dignity of his aim and the natural command inherent in a lofty spirit. This deceit was the beginning of his decadence, which ended in a sad self-aggrandizement, when he felt himself no longer an instrument of intuition to probe the secrets of the earth, but a possessor of miraculous inspiration. The man who had been self-contained became a thrall to a fevered hallucination.

The earnest mental study which had sustained his inquisitive spirit through long years of dealings with the great physical problems of the earth was forgotten. He hopelessly began to accredit to Divinity the measure of his own fallibility. "God made me," he says, "the messenger of the new heaven and the new earth, of which He spoke in the Apocalypse by St. John, after having spoken of it by the mouth of Isaiah, and He showed me the spot where to find it." He no longer thought it the views of Aristotle which guided him. The Greek might be pardoned for his ignorance of the intervening America. It was mere sacrilege to impute such ignorance to the Divine wisdom. . . .

We have seen a pitiable man meet a pitiable death. Hardly a name in profane history is more august than his. Hardly another character in the world's record has made so little of its opportunities. His discovery was a blunder; his blunder was a new world; the New World is his monument! Its discoverer might have been its father; he proved to be its despoiler. He might have given its young days such a benignity as the world likes to associate with a maker; he left it a legacy of devastation and crime. He might have been an unselfish promoter of geographical science; he proved a rabid seeker for gold and a viceroyalty. He might have won converts to the fold of Christ by the kindness of his spirit; he gained the execrations of the good angels.

Hardly another character in the world's record has made so little of its opportunities. His discovery was a blunder.

He might, like Las Casas, have rebuked the fiendishness of his contemporaries; he set them an example of perverted belief. The triumph of Barcelona led down to the ignominy of Valladolid, with every step in the degradation palpable and resultant.

3

Modern Attacks on Columbus Are Unwarranted

Mark Falcoff

Mark Falcoff, a resident scholar at the American Enterpise Institute, writes on Latin American politics, U.S. foreign policy, and intelligence policy. In the following viewpoint, Falcoff argues that the vicious attacks on Columbus, which include blaming him for a host of ills, are for the most part historically inaccurate and unfounded.

U ntil quite recently, Columbus's arrival in what is now the Dominican Republic on October 12, 1492, was unambiguously regarded as one of the most important—and fortuitous—events in history. And Columbus himself, part mystic and dreamer, part man of science, part arbitrageur, has long embodied qualities particularly attractive to Americans. "The pioneer of progress and enlightenment" was the way President Benjamin Harrison described Columbus when he opened the celebrations marking the fourth century since the voyage. What followed in 1892 was a vast orgy of self-congratulation that lasted a full year, punctuated by brass bands, the Columbian Exposition in Chicago, even the commissioning of Dvorak's New World Symphony.

Every age tends to rewrite history according to its own needs and prejudices, so a repetition of the 1892 commemoration was unlikely. Given the temper of our times and the

Abridged from Mark Falcoff, "Was 1492 a Mistake?" *The American Enterprise*, January/February 1992. Copyright © 1992 The American Enterprise. Distributed by The New York Times Special Features/Syndication Sales. Reprinted with permission.

particular drift that elite culture has taken in the United States, uncritical accolades were hardly to be expected. Even so, some of the indisputable consequences of Columbus's achievement—the sudden, radical enlargement of geographical knowledge, the transcontinental exchange of plants and animals, the incorporation of a huge portion of the earth into a larger economic system, the birth of new nations and cultures, even the widening of the political and moral horizons of humanity—would seem to be worthy of appreciation by even our most skeptical contemporaries. In fact, . . . Columbus and his legacy have come under an attack from a coalition of religious, cultural, and racial groups.

The struggle over historical meaning began with words. The term "discovery" has suddenly become suspect because it seems to indicate that the indigenous peoples of this hemisphere existed only after Europeans became aware of them. Stated that way, who could disagree? But finding another word to substitute for "discovery" proved to be surprisingly difficult. Only after extensive negotiations was the Columbus Quincentenary Commission in the United States able to convince its critics to accept a compromise: we are now to regard what happened in 1492 not as a "discovery" at all but as an "encounter." Encounter sounds agreeably neutral since it places both the discoverer and the discovered on an apparent plane of cultural equality. But it fails to convey the full richness of the event; clearly, something is missing. Columnist John Leo recently quipped, "'Encounter'—as in, 'My car has encountered a large truck going 80 miles an hour.'"

The struggle over terms masks deeper emotions. After all, those who are trying to consign the word "discovery" to oblivion have not set out to merely establish cultural parity between two worlds; rather, they hope to advance a more radical social and historical vision. The United Nations discovered this as long ago as 1986 when, after four years of impassioned debate, it abandoned altogether any attempt to celebrate the event. Here in the United States, the lead has been taken by the National Council of Churches, which refers to 1492 and all of the events that followed as "an invasion and colonization . . . with genocide, economic exploitation, and a deep level of institutional racism and moral decadence."

Historical Revisionism

With an even broader brush, the American Library Association classifies the entire period of the European discovery and colonization of the Western hemisphere as the "Native American Holocaust" and urges its members to approach the Columbus celebrations "from an authentic Native American perspective, dealing directly with topics like cultural imperialism [and] colonialism." Author Kirkpatrick Sale, whose new book about Columbus, *The Conquest of Paradise*, has appeared just in time to benefit from the new "revisionist" wave, prefers to condemn the Great Mariner for "ecocide"—the destruction of the delicate balance between man and nature that presumably existed before his arrival.

Not surprisingly, leaders of indigenous communities in the United States have contributed much to this discussion. According to Russell Means of the American Indian Movement (AIM), Columbus "makes Hitler look like a juvenile delinquent." Suzan Shoan Haijo [*sic*: Shown Harjo] of the Morning Star Foundation, a member of the Cheyenne-Creek and Arapaho Indian nations, urges us to commemorate instead the five-hundredth anniversary of *1491*, which she calls "the last *good* year." As Garry Wills recently put it, "A funny thing happened on the way to the quincentennial celebration of America's discovery . . . Columbus got mugged. This time the Indians were waiting for him." A headline summarizes the situation telegraphically: "Columbus, a Ruthless Racist Now, Sails Toward Public Relations Reef."

Columbus's Early Critics

The sudden tidal wave of resistance to the Columbus celebrations might be the product of new information about the man, his life, and his works, but in fact it is not. Most of what we know today was known by earlier generations 100, possibly even 200, years ago. There have always been arguments about Columbus's ancestry as well as whether he really was the first European mariner to discover this hemisphere. (Lately, there have been assertions that not Columbus but African sailors first established the translantic link between the two hemispheres.) But the circumstances of Columbus's voyages as well as the short- and longer-term impacts have never been in doubt, including all of the unlovely aspects: the virtual obliteration of some Indian populations, the enslavement of others, and the subsequent decision to import African chattels to supplement the colonial labor force.

The controversy over the moral dimension of the European conquest is likewise not new. It was initiated more than 400 years ago by a Spaniard, Bartolomé de las Casas. A soldier and settler in Cuba and Hispaniola before taking Dominican orders, Las Casas was the first person in Western history to clearly raise the issue of the rights of the conquered indigenous peoples. As a demographer, he left something to be desired, but as a propagandist he displayed uncommon imagination, verve, and what today we would call public relations sense. He managed to get a hearing at the special levee of the Spanish court specifically convoked in Valladolid in 1550 to resolve the most controversial issue of the day: whether the Indians of the newly discovered lands possessed immortal souls and therefore deserved the same treatment as other men. There Las Casas took on Juan Ginés de Sepúlveda, one of the most learned advocates in Europe, who had been retained by the Spanish-settler community in America. Though the great debate ended in a draw, the Spanish monarchy, influenced by Las Casas's arguments, finally abolished Indian servitude in its overseas provinces—a command that was unenforced and also, unfortunately, ultimately unenforceable.

Las Casas's real contribution, however, was not legal but ideological and historiographic. His *Brief History of the Destruction of the Indies*, published in 1550–1551, was the first human rights report in history. It recounted in exquisite detail incidents of torture, murder, and mistreatment of the native populations by ruthless Spanish adventurers. In effect, Las Casas accused his fellow countrymen of nothing less than genocide. Translated almost immediately into the major European languages and published under the new title *Tears of the Indies*, his book became an international best-seller. Outside the Iberian peninsula, it generated an entire literature of indictment of Spain and all things Spanish. In fact, it became the cornerstone of the Black Legend, the enduring notion—particularly in Northern European countries but also in the United States and to some degree even in Latin America—that Spaniards are uniquely cruel, bigoted, tyrannical, obscurantist, lazy, fanatical, greedy, and treacherous. Las Casas's work thus marks the point of departure for another, singularly Western phenomenon: the penchant for certain strains of national self-criticism to pass, sometimes imperceptibly, over into national self-hatred.

Nor is the notion of pre-Columbian America as Paradise Lost something only now being discovered by our environmentalists. Columbus's own journals make reference to the innocence and primitive charm of the Indians who approached his caravels ("naked as their mothers bore them") and to the abundance of their natural environment. The concept of the "noble savage" dominates Las Casas's work. Even Spaniards who actually participated in the conquests of Mexico and Peru thought much the same at first; fascinated by the complexity and sophistication of the societies they encountered, some found themselves grasping for metaphors drawn from the Spanish books of chivalry, the closest thing they possessed to utopian literature. . . .

What We Know Now

It is easier to forgive eighteenth-century Europeans for playing loose with the facts about pre-Columbian America than it is to excuse some of our contemporaries. After all, the former did not have the benefit of the modern disciplines of history, anthropology, and archaeology. In his *Brief History*, Las Casas claimed that the Spaniards had killed 20 million Indians in the process of settling Hispaniola and the other islands of the archipelago. Today, we know that Columbus and his men could not have done this even if they had tried. As historian John Tate Lanning pointed out some years ago, "If each Spaniard listed in Bermúdez Plata's *Passengers to the Indies*" for a half century after the discovery "had killed an Indian every day and three on Sunday, it would have taken a generation to do the job."

The issue, of course, is not just one of numbers, although perhaps it bears repeating here that exterminating Indians was decidedly not the purpose of the conquest. The Spaniards had no interest whatever in reducing the numbers of their potential labor force or, for that matter, the number of potential converts to Catholic Christianity. In arriving at his figures, Las Casas and many others who followed in his tradition did not allow for the diminution of the Indian populations by simple circumstance: their lack of immunity to European diseases, warfare with other tribes, culture shock, and even miscegenation—that is, the gradual integration into the newer and larger racially mixed communities created by Spanish settlements in the late sixteenth and early seventeenth centuries.

Nor is what we now know about some of the more important Indian societies particularly reassuring, at least for those who claim to hold in high regard such things as harmony with nature or respect for cultural and political pluralism. The Aztecs were a people of remarkable attainments—authors of a civilization that merits our admiration even now, nearly four centuries after its extinction—but they were an imperial race that had conquered and subordinated most of the other peoples of the Valley of Mexico and waged relentless war upon their neighbors to extract victims for human sacrifice to continually appease the gods.

By the time the Spaniards reached what is now Central America, the Mayan civilization there had been in decline for several hundred years. Until very recently, archaeologists were mystified by the apparent sudden disappearance of a federation of Mayan temple-cities around 900 A.D., since they believed that the Mayans had been a peaceful and philosophical people—accomplished artists, poets, and astronomers. But now, the first commemorative stones have been deciphered, and we know otherwise. There was no federation in the first place, nor could there have been one, because the Mayans were every bit as aggressive and warlike as the Aztecs. But at some point, things veered out of control, and stylized warfare between kings degenerated into large-scale attacks on each other's cities, devastation of agricultural fields, and the wholesale murder of innocent civilians.

In North America, the Indians were far less sophisticated than the Aztecs or the Mayans. Human sacrifice did not play a role in their religious life, but it cannot be said that they were particularly respectful of the environment, except insofar as their small numbers and their primitive level of technology made it difficult to leave much of a mark on the lands they occupied. Many lived a seminomadic existence as hunter-gatherers, moving on after the most obvious and immediate natural resources were becoming depleted. Nor were they, by and large, respectful of other Indian peoples, whom they considered as alien as the white man. From what we know about these societies—and we know quite a lot—ideas like minority rights and pluralism played no role in their political, or rather prepolitical, organization.

Despite this, we hear that the Indian peoples of the Americas—past and present—constitute a peerless repository of virtues. When examined more carefully, however, these turn out to be Western virtues, and uniquely Western virtues at that. This, surely, is the message of Kevin Costner's updated horse opera, *Dances with Wolves*. The question is indiscreet, but the "revisionists" do not allow us to avoid it: Are indigenous peoples better practitioners of Western values than the West? Alas, there is not much evidence that they are or were. And it is as unfair to them as it is to us to pretend otherwise.

With the best will in the world, it is simply not possible to be historically honest and at the same time credit them with achievements that parallel those of our Founding Fathers in Philadelphia.

The Central Paradox

Nothing we know and nothing we are likely to learn will ever justify to our contemporaries the conquest of other peoples—no matter how primitive or brutal those people were. That is the point first made by Father Las Casas, and it is crucial to the development of the modern Western sensibility. But to debate these issues as if they are part of ongoing events completely upsets the applecart of context. Las Casas wrote at a time when there was still some hope of shaping native policy in the Spanish colonies. Today, the Columbus controversy is not about what to do but (at least by indirection) about what should have been done. In so doing, the revisionists force the rest of us to follow their argument to its "logical" conclusion. If the European discovery of America was indeed "an invasion of colonization . . . with genocide, economic exploitation, and a deep level of institutional racism and moral decadence," then there can be only one historical conclusion: 1492 was a mistake. Columbus went too far. And to this there can be only one solution—we must all mount our boats and return from whence we came.

There is another troubling contradiction in the critics' bill of indictment: How seriously can we take accusations of genocide, ecocide, and other disasters nothing less than cosmic when the remedies counseled are at best meliorative and incremental? The best that the more serious-minded can manage is a year-long program of reflection and repentance. In this spirit, Professor Franklin B. Knight of Johns

Hopkins University instructs us to "educate ourselves about a brave new world devoid of the arrogance and ethnocentrism of the past, in which all people are taken on their own terms and accorded dignity and respect—the rich as well as the poor, the developed as well as the underdeveloped, the mighty and the weak, the large and the small."

Today's Focus

These and other incongruities do not trouble Columbus's contemporary critics because they are really not much interested in what happened in 1492 or even the centuries thereafter. Theirs is a distemper with the world in which we live today. Having failed thus far to sell on the open market their political agenda—slow-growth or no-growth, an incomes policy based on imagined grievances rather than productivity, and redistribution of resources based on racial spoils—they are now trying to bludgeon it home on the cultural battlefield. The Columbus controversy is merely the latest engagement in this war.

By selecting this particular issue, the revisionists and their allies have shown a certain panache. They have already managed to turn what might have been a rather dull, pro forma observance into something more controversial and even newsworthy, and before the quincentennial year is over, they will doubtless have done still more: by leveraging the machinery of our sensitive political system; by intimidating university administrators, museum directors, and librarians; by threatening unseemly public demonstrations; and by straining this country's apparently inexhaustible fund of patience, tolerance, and basic decency. But will they succeed in what after all is their large objective—to change the way we feel about ourselves, our country, and the larger civilization of which we are a part? Not likely.

But even without intending to do so, they have raised some questions that are entirely appropriate to the quincentennial year and also to the ongoing cultural debate in our own country. According to what standards can the West be held accountable for the actions that accompanied its discovery and settlement of the Americas? The only possible answer would seem to be—its own. Do we know today something we did not know yesterday that puts in a morally inferior light the spread of European culture to the Western hemisphere? We do not. In a larger sense, has the spread of

European civilization around the globe, not just in this hemisphere, been on balance a positive factor in world history? There can be no doubt that it has.

In its particulars, the Iberian conquest of the Americas in no way differed from the course of other empires in world history, replete with murder, exploitation, forced relocation of populations, and the destruction of whole cultures. But its moral framework was radically dissimilar. Yes, it was Spaniards who committed the abuses and crimes of the conquest, but it was also Spaniards, as the distinguished Peruvian novelist Mario Vargas Llosa has reminded us, who were the first to condemn those abuses and demand that they be brought to an end, "abandon[ing] the ranks in order to collaborate with the vanquished.". . .

For even the harshest critics of our societies in this hemisphere cannot deny that over these past 500 years— and particularly the last 200—we have not exactly wallowed in complacency and self-satisfaction. After all, the Americas were the birthplace of the revolutionary ideas of political self-determination and the economic autonomy of the individual. Those who imagine that these are antiquated nineteenth-century notions that have outlived their relevance must face the fact that today they are now spreading around the world, even to such unlikely corners as Albania and China. Admittedly, this is not what Columbus had in mind when he set sail from Huelva thinking he would eventually drop anchor in the harbors of the Great Khan, but without his journey in the first place, the history of humanity might have been very different—and very much darker.

The Iberian conquest of the Americas in no way differed from the course of other empires in world history, replete with . . . the destruction of whole cultures.

Nor is this merely a matter of historical speculation. We can, in fact, test the proposition. The entire period since 1945 has been one long orgy of anticolonialism throughout much of Africa and Asia and of milder forms of anti-Western sentiment in much of Latin America. What we have learned from recent experience in these places is that where Western ideas and values have declined or been expelled, there is less freedom, not more; less human dignity; less food; less education; poorer health—in short, regression, not progress.

The failure of anti-Western ideologies in Cuba and Angola, in Vietnam and Mozambique, in Algeria, Syria, and Iraq, ought to give greater pause to the critics of Western civilization currently trying to hitch a free ride home on Columbus's caravels.

Without his journey in the first place, the history of humanity might have been very different—and very much darker.

On one point, the critics of Columbus are not wrong: his voyage is indeed a proper metaphor for the spread of Western influence throughout the world. That influence is once again on the rise, this time not inadvertently but by the sheer force of its ideas. As Western civilization approaches a universal ideal, the distinction between discoverers and the discovered will become meaningless. And 100 years from now, the Columbus controversy will seem even more bizarre and incomprehensible than it does today.

4

Modern Attacks on Columbus Are Justified

Suzan Shown Harjo

Suzan Shown Harjo, a Cheyenne-Creek, is president and director of the Morning Star Foundation in Washington, D.C. The foundation sponsored the 1992 Alliance, a vehicle for "indigenous peoples' response to the Columbus Quincentenary." In the following viewpoint, Harjo explains why modern attacks on Columbus are necessary to eradicate injustice.

Why aren't you joining in the celebrations of the Columbus quincentenary?

As Native American peoples in this red quarter of Mother Earth, we have no reason to celebrate an invasion that caused the demise of so many of our people and is still causing destruction today. The Europeans stole our land and killed our people.

But because the quincentenary is a cause celebre, it provides an opportunity to put forth Native American perspectives on the next 500 years.

Columbus was just "a man of his times." Why are you so critical of him? Why not look at the positive aspects of his legacy?

For people who are in survival mode, it's very difficult to look at the positive aspects of death and destruction, especially when it is carried through to our present. There is a reason we are the poorest people in America. There is a reason we have the highest teen suicide rate. There is a reason why our people are ill-housed and in poor health, and we do not live as long as the majority population.

From "We Have No Reason to Celebrate an Invasion," an interview with Barbara Miner, by Suzan Shown Harjo, *Rethinking Schools*, October/November 1991. Used with permission.

That reason has to do with the fact that we were in the way of Western civilization and we were in the way of westward expansion. We suffered the "excesses" of civilization such as murder, pillage, rape, destruction of the major waterways, destruction of land, the destruction and pollution of the air.

We have no reason to celebrate an invasion that caused the demise of so many of our people and is still causing destruction today.

What are those "positive" aspects of the Columbus legacy? If we're talking about the horse, yeah, that's good. We like the horse. Indians raised the use of the horse to high military art, especially among the Cheyenne people and the tribes of the plains states.

Was that a good result of that invasion? Yes. Is it something we would have traded for the many Indian peoples who are no longer here because of that invasion? No.

We also like the beads that came from Europe, and again we raised their use to a high art. Would we have traded those beads for the massacres of our people, such as the Sand Creek massacre [in which U.S. soldiers massacred hundreds of Native American men, women, and children at Sand Creek, Colorado, in 1864]? No.

Why do we focus on Columbus rather than any number of U.S. presidents who were also responsible for the death and destruction of Indian people? Because it's his 500 years; it's his quincentenary.

Isn't criticism of Columbus a form of picking on the Spaniards? Were they any worse than other Europeans who came to America?

In my estimation, the Spaniards were no worse than any number of other Europeans. The economy of slavery and serfdom that existed in northern Europe—how do you measure that in cruelty and in long-term effects against the Spanish Inquisition?

I view the issue more as the oppressive nature and arrogance of the Christian religions. And that continues today.

Our Indian religions are not missionary religions. We are taught to respect other religions. It was a shock when we were met with proselytizing zealots, especially those who thought that if your soul can't be saved, you're better off dead—or if your soul can be saved, you should be dead so you can go to heaven. And that's the history of that original encounter.

Arrogance and Ignorance

How does that arrogance and ignorance manifest itself today?

How? Well, for example, the Catholic Church has said that 1992 is a time to enter into a period of grace and healing and to celebrate the evangelization of the Americas. My word, how can you be graceful and healing about the tens of thousands of native people who were killed because they would not convert to a religion they didn't understand, or because they didn't understand the language of those making the request?

We were in the way of Western civilization and we were in the way of westward expansion.

It's difficult to take seriously an apology that is not coupled with atonement. It's as if they're saying, "I'm sorry, oops, and we'll be better in the next hemisphere." That doesn't cut it. We've had empty platitudes before.

The combination of arrogance and ignorance also results in making mascots of Indian people, of dehumanizing and stereotyping them—in the sports world, in advertising, and in society at large. The Washington Redskins football team is an excellent example.

There is no more derogatory name in English for Indian people than the name Redskins. And the Redskins is a prominent image right here in the nation's capital that goes by unnoticed. Because we are an invisible population, the racism against us is also invisible for the most part.

You don't see sports teams called the White Trash, the Black Chicks, the Jew Boys, or the Jack Mormons. And if we did see that, it wouldn't be for long, you can be sure of that.

Why can't we use the Columbus quincentenary to celebrate American diversity and the contributions of all, Europeans and Native Americans alike?

There will be lots of people who will be putting forth

the perspective of rah rah Columbus, rah rah Western Civilization. Our perspective is putting forth native peoples' views on our past and present. We also want to get into the public consciousness the notion that we actually have a future on this planet. This is something missed by even what is hailed as the most progressive of American movies, *Dances with Wolves.*

We're more interested in the 500 years before Columbus and what will go on in the next 500 years. The truth of the intervening 500 years is really known in the hearts of people worldwide, even though the particulars have been obscured by a cotton-candy version of history.

Aren't some of the criticisms of Columbus just substituting Native-centrism for Euro-centrism?

Oppressed people need to be centered within themselves. Racism and centrism become a problem if you are in the dominant society and are subjugating other people as a result of your centrism. I don't accept the question. I think it's an empty argument.

Aren't criticisms of Columbus just another form of insuring "political correctness"?

The Eurocentric view, having been exposed for its underlying falsehood, now wishes to oppose any other view as either equally false or simply the flip side of reality: a secondary or dual reality.

It was a shock when we [Native Americans] met with proselytizing zealots, especially those who thought that if your soul can't be saved, you're better off dead.

Feelings are usually dual realities; perspectives are dual realities. But there are some things that don't have a dual reality. For example, if we look at who has polluted all of our water, causing a whole lot of death and whole lot of illness in this country alone, then we have a bit of a clue where the problem might rest. We have a clue whose reality might expose the truth and whose reality might obscure the truth.

It's about time for the people who are the true historic revisionists, who are on the far right side of this whole political correctness debate, to stop lying to themselves, to their readership and to their students. They must stop their silly ivory tower kinds of debates about whether multiculturalism should be used, and so forth.

What is the true history? Just start dealing with some undisputable realities. The world is a mess. This country is a mess. The people who fare the worst in this country are poor, non-white children and poor, non-white old people. Societies who do not care for their young people and old people are decadent, decaying societies.

I think there are a lot of good minds that are reflecting that decadence and decay when they choose to spend their time on these kinds of ivory tower debates. There are things about which they can do much, and they are doing nothing.

What are the key struggles that native people face today?

We need, in the first instance, basic human rights such as religious freedom. Or how about life, liberty and the pursuit of happiness, and other things that many people in the United States view as standard fare but are out of reach for Indian people?

There is also the issue of land and treaty rights. We have property that we don't own and we should, and we have property that we own that we don't control and we should.

We have treaties with the United States that are characterized in the U.S. Constitution as the supreme law of the land. Yet every one, without exception, of nearly 400 treaties signed between native peoples and the U.S. government has been broken. Every one of them.

A good place to start would be for the United States to live up to every treaty agreement. It's also the way you get at resolving some of the problems of poverty, alcoholism, unemployment, and poor health.

If we don't handle the big things, we can't get to the manifestations of the problem. We have to go to the basic human rights issues, the basic treaty rights issues.

If we don't resolve these issues, then all people in this country are going to be complicit in the continuing effort to wipe out our Indian people. It's as simple as that.

Chapter 2

The Conquistadors

1

The Conquistadors
Were Murderers

Bartolomé de las Casas

Bartolomé de las Casas, born in 1474, became known as an advocate of Indian rights. In 1492 las Casas was beginning legal and theological studies at the University of Salamanca. His father and uncle accompanied Columbus on the second voyage. The younger las Casas went to the New World originally as a colonist. He knew personally many of the leaders of the conquest—Cortés, Pizarro, and Alvarado, and accompanied Diego Velásquez and Panfilo de Narváez in the "pacification" of Cuba in 1512. Renouncing his possessions and slaves, las Casas was ordained. He spent most of the rest of his life—from 1514 on—defending the Indians against extermination. In addition to writing the *Apologetic History of the Indies* and the *General History of the Indies*, las Casas systematically collected manuscripts, letters, and official documents referring to the conquest of America. Without him, we would not have Columbus's ships' logs, for he preserved a transcript of those documents in his archives. He returned to Madrid for the last time in 1547. One of his last public acts was a debate in Vallodolid with Ginés de Sepúlveda in 1550 over whether the conquest of Indian lands and the war against the Indians were justified. Las Casas vehemently argued no. Las Casas died in 1566, writing in defense of the Indians until the very last.

The Indies were discovered in the year one thousand four hundred and ninety-two. In the following year a great many Spaniards went there with the intention of set-

From *The Devastation of the Indies: A Brief Account*, by Bartolomé de las Casas, translated by Herma Briffault (New York: Seabury Press, 1974). Copyright © 1974 by Seabury Press and The Continuum Publishing Group. Reprinted by permission of the publisher.

tling the land. Thus, forty-nine years have passed since the first settlers penetrated the land, the first so-claimed being the large and most happy isle called Hispaniola, which is six hundred leagues in circumference. Around it in all directions are many other islands, some very big, others very small, and all of them were, as we saw with our own eyes, densely populated with native peoples called Indians. This large island was perhaps the most densely populated place in the world. There must be close to two hundred leagues of land on this island, and the seacoast has been explored for more than ten thousand leagues, and each day more of it is being explored. And all the land so far discovered is a beehive of people; it is as though God had crowded into these lands the great majority of mankind.

A Description of the Indians

And of all the infinite universe of humanity, these people are the most guileless, the most devoid of wickedness and duplicity, the most obedient and faithful to their native masters and to the Spanish Christians whom they serve. They are by nature the most humble, patient, and peaceable, holding no grudges, free from embroilments, neither excitable nor quarrelsome. These people are the most devoid of rancors, hatreds, or desire for vengeance of any people in the world. And because they are so weak and complaisant, they are less able to endure heavy labor and soon die of no matter what malady. The sons of nobles among us, brought up in the enjoyments of life's refinements, are no more delicate than are these Indians, even those among them who are of the lowest rank of laborers. They are also poor people, for they not only possess little but have no desire to possess worldly goods. For this reason they are not arrogant, embittered, or greedy. Their repasts are such that the food of the holy fathers in the desert can scarcely be more parsimonious, scanty, and poor. As to their dress, they are generally naked, with only their pudenda covered somewhat. And when they cover their shoulders it is with a square cloth no more than two varas in size. They have no beds, but sleep on a kind of matting or else in a kind of suspended net called *hamacas*. They are very clean in their persons, with alert, intelligent minds, docile and open to doctrine, very apt to receive our holy Catholic faith, to be endowed with virtuous customs, and to behave in a godly fashion. And once they begin to hear the tidings of the Faith, they are so insistent on knowing more and on taking the sacraments of the Church and on observing the divine cult that, truly, the missionaries who are here need to be endowed by God with great patience in order to cope with such eagerness. Some of the secular Spaniards who have been here for many years say that the goodness of the Indians is undeniable and that if this gifted people could be brought to know the one true God they would be the most fortunate people in the world.

Ravening Wild Beasts

Yet into this sheepfold, into this land of meek outcasts there came some Spaniards who immediately behaved like ravening wild beasts, wolves, tigers, or lions that had been starved for many days. And Spaniards have behaved in no other way during the past forty years, down to the present time, for they are still acting like ravening beasts, killing, terrorizing, afflicting, torturing, and destroying the native peoples, doing all this with the strangest and most varied new methods of cruelty, never seen or heard of before, and to such a degree that this Island of Hispaniola, once so populous (having a population that I estimated to be more than three millions), has now a population of barely two hundred persons.

The island of Cuba is nearly as long as the distance between Valladolid and Rome; it is now almost completely depopulated. San Juan and Jamaica are two of the largest, most productive and attractive islands; both are now deserted and devastated. On the northern side of Cuba and Hispaniola lie the neighboring Lucayos comprising more than sixty islands including those called *Gigantes*, beside numerous other islands, some small some large. The least felicitous of them were more fertile and beautiful than the gardens of the King of Seville. They have the healthiest lands in the world, where lived more than five hundred thousand souls; they are now deserted, inhabited by not a single living creature. All the people were slain or died after being taken into captivity and brought to the Island of Hispaniola to be sold as slaves. When the Spaniards saw that some of these had escaped, they sent a ship to find them, and it voyaged for three years among the islands searching for those who had escaped being slaughtered, for a good Christian had helped them escape, taking pity on them and had won them over to Christ; of these there were eleven persons and these I saw.

Ruin and Depopulation

More than thirty other islands in the vicinity of San Juan are for the most part and for the same reason depopulated, and the land laid waste. On these islands I estimate there are 2,100 leagues of land that have been ruined and depopulated, empty of people.

As for the vast mainland, which is ten times larger than all Spain, even including Aragon and Portugal, containing more land than the distance between Seville and Jerusalem, or more than two thousand leagues, we are sure that our Spaniards, with their cruel and abominable acts, have devastated the land and exterminated the rational people who fully inhabited it. We can estimate very surely and truthfully that in the forty years that have passed, with the infernal actions of the Christians, there have been unjustly slain more than twelve million men, women, and children. In truth, I believe without trying to deceive myself that the number of the slain is more like fifteen million.

The common ways mainly employed by the Spaniards who call themselves Christian and who have gone there to extirpate those pitiful nations and wipe them off the earth is by unjustly waging cruel and bloody wars. Then, when they have slain all those who fought for their lives or to escape the tortures they would have to endure, that is to say, when they have slain all the native rulers and young men (since the Spaniards usually spare only the women and children, who are subjected to the hardest and bitterest servitude ever suffered by man or beast), they enslave any survivors. With these infernal methods of tyranny they debase and weaken countless numbers of those pitiful Indian nations.

A Wish for Gold

Their reason for killing and destroying such an infinite number of souls is that the Christians have an ultimate aim, which is to acquire gold, and to swell themselves with riches in a very brief time and thus rise to a high estate disproportionate to their merits. It should be kept in mind that their insatiable greed and ambition, the greatest ever seen in the world, is the cause of their villainies. And also, those lands are so rich and felicitous, the native peoples so meek and patient, so easy to subject, that our Spaniards have no more consideration for them than beasts. And I say this from my own knowledge of the acts I witnessed. But I should not say "than beasts" for, thanks be to God, they have treated beasts with some respect; I should say instead like excrement on the public squares. And thus they have deprived the Indians of their lives and souls, for the millions I mentioned have died without the Faith and without the benefit of the sacraments. This is a well-known and proven fact which even the tyrant Governors, themselves killers, know and admit. And never have the Indians in all the Indies committed any act against the Spanish Christians, until those Christians have first and many times committed countless cruel aggressions against them or against neighboring nations. For in the beginning the Indians regarded the Spaniards as angels from Heaven. Only after the Spaniards had used violence against them, killing, robbing, torturing, did the Indians ever rise up against them.

[The Spaniards] took infants from their mothers' breasts, snatching them by the legs and pitching them headfirst against the crags.

On the Island Hispaniola was where the Spaniards first landed, as I have said. Here those Christians perpetrated their first ravages and oppressions against the native peoples. This was the first land in the New World to be destroyed and depopulated by the Christians, and here they began their subjection of the women and children, taking them away from the Indians to use them and ill use them, eating the food they provided with their sweat and toil. The Spaniards did not content themselves with what the Indians gave them of their own free will, according to their ability, which was always too little to satisfy enormous appetites, for a Christian eats and consumes in one day an amount of food that would suffice to feed three houses inhabited by ten Indians for one month. And they committed other acts of force and violence and oppression which made the Indians realize that these men had not come from Heaven. And some of the Indians concealed their foods while others concealed their wives and children and still others fled to the mountains to avoid the terrible transactions of the Christians.

And the Christians attacked them with buffets and beatings, until finally they laid hands on the nobles of the villages. Then they behaved with such temerity and shamelessness that the most powerful ruler of the islands had to see his own wife raped by a Christian officer.

From that time onward the Indians began to seek ways to throw the Christians out of their lands. They took up arms, but their weapons were very weak and of little service in offense and still less in defense. (Because of this, the wars of the Indians against each other are little more than games played by children.) And the Christians, with their horses and swords and pikes began to carry out massacres and strange cruelties against them. They attacked the towns and spared neither the children nor the aged nor pregnant women nor women in childbed, not only stabbing them and dismembering them but cutting them to pieces as if dealing with sheep in the slaughter house. They laid bets as to who, with one stroke of the sword, could split a man in two or could cut off his head or spill out his entrails with a single stroke of the pike. They took infants from their mothers' breasts, snatching them by the legs and pitching them headfirst against the crags or snatched them by the arms and threw them into the rivers, roaring with laughter and saying as the babies fell into the water, "Boil there, you offspring of the devil!" Other infants they put to the sword along with their mothers and anyone else who happened to be nearby. They made some low wide gallows on which the hanged victim's feet almost touched the ground, stringing up their victims in lots of thirteen, in memory of Our Redeemer and His twelve Apostles, then set burning wood at their feet and thus burned them alive. To others they attached straw or wrapped their whole bodies in straw and set them afire. With still others, all those they wanted to capture alive, they cut off their hands and hung them round the victim's neck, saying, "Go now, carry the message," meaning, Take the news to the Indians who have fled to the mountains. They usually dealt with the chieftains and nobles in the following way: they made a grid of rods which they placed on forked sticks, then lashed the victims to the grid and lighted a smoldering fire underneath, so that little by little, as those captives screamed in despair and torment, their souls would leave them.

Incredible Brutality

I once saw this, when there were four or five nobles lashed on grids and burning; I seem even to recall that there were two or three pairs of grids where others were burning, and because they uttered such loud screams that they disturbed the captain's sleep, he ordered them to be strangled. And the constable, who was worse than an executioner, did not want to obey that order (and I know the name of that constable and know his relatives in Seville), but instead put a stick over the victims' tongues, so they could not make a sound, and he stirred up the fire, but not too much, so that they roasted slowly, as he liked. I saw all these things I have described, and countless others.

And because all the people who could do so fled to the mountains to escape these inhuman, ruthless, and ferocious acts, the Spanish captains, enemies of the human race, pursued them with the fierce dogs they kept which attacked the Indians, tearing them to pieces and devouring them. And because on few and far between occasions, the Indians justifiably killed some Christians, the Spaniards made a rule among themselves that for every Christian slain by the Indians, they would slay a hundred Indians. . . .

Wicked and Cruel by Nature

Among the noteworthy outrages they committed was the one they perpetrated against a cacique, a very important noble, by name Hatuey, who had come to Cuba from Hispaniola with many of his people, to flee the calamities and inhuman acts of the Christians. When he was told by certain Indians that the Christians were now coming to Cuba, he assembled as many of his followers as he could and said this to them: "Now you must know that they are saying the Christians are coming here, and you know by experience how they put So and So and So and So, and other nobles to an end. And now they are coming from Haiti (which is Hispaniola) to do the same here. Do you know why they do this?" The Indians replied: "We do not know. But it may be that they are by nature wicked and cruel." And he told them: "No, they do not act only because of that, but because they have a God they greatly worship and they want us to worship that God, and that is why they struggle with us and subject us and kill us."

He had a basket full of gold and jewels and he said: "You see their God here, the God of the Christians. If you agree to it, let us dance for this God, who knows, it may please the God of the Christians and then they will do us no harm."

And his followers said, all together, "Yes, that is good, that is good!" And they danced round the basket of gold until they fell down exhausted. Then their chief, the cacique Hatuey, said to them: "See here, if we keep this basket of gold they will take it from us and will end up by killing us. So let us cast away the basket into the river." They all agreed to do this, and they flung the basket of gold into the river that was nearby.

This cacique, Hatuey, was constantly fleeing before the Christians from the time they arrived on the island of Cuba, since he knew them and of what they were capable. Now and then they encountered him and he defended himself, but they finally killed him. And they did this for the sole reason that he had fled from those cruel and wicked Christians and had defended himself against them. And when they had captured him and as many of his followers as they could, they burned them all at the stake.

When tied to the stake, the cacique Hatuey was told by a Franciscan friar who was present, an artless rascal, something about the God of the Christians and of the articles of the Faith. And he was told what he could do in the brief time that remained to him, in order to be saved and go to Heaven. The cacique, who had never heard any of this before, and was told he would go to Inferno where if he did not adopt the Christian Faith, he would suffer eternal torment, asked the Franciscan friar if Christians all went to Heaven. When told that they did he said he would prefer to go to Hell. Such is the fame and honor that God and our Faith have earned through the Christians who have gone out to the Indies.

2

The Conquistadors' Motives Were Pure

Jean Descola

Jean Descola, a Parisian by birth, clearly is a Hispanophile. Unlike many English writers, he is far more sympathetic to the conquistadors, perhaps because Spain was never a national enemy to the French to the same degree it was to the English and Dutch. Much of Descola's writing has been on Spain and Latin America. *The Conquistadors*, from which the following viewpoint is excerpted, won a major French literary prize, Le Grand Prix d'Histoire.

The Conquistador resembles no one but himself. He is a Spaniard, the product of the conquering and mystical Spain of the sixteenth century, made in its image, and reflecting the somber glory of its contradictory passions. He carries in himself, with a sort of terrible ingenuity, the whole of Spain. He *is* Spain. And just as we cannot define in one word, or reduce to a single formula, the historic face of Charles V's Spain, so we must consider successively the various aspects of the Conquistador, so that a true portrait may emerge, one removed both from the "black legend" and from the romantic image.

Neither Saints nor Bandits

Here are a few judgments on the Conquistadors. Heinrich Heine was categorical: "They were bandits," he said. Angel Canivet claims that they conquered "by spontaneous necessity, by virtue of a natural impulse toward independence,

From *The Conquistadores*, by Jean Descola, translated by Malcolm Barnes. Copyright © 1957 by the Viking Press; renewed © 1985 by Viking Penguin, Inc. Used by permission of Viking Penguin, a division of Penguin Putnam Inc.

without other purpose than to reveal the grandeur which hid itself beneath their apparent smallness." Maurice Legendre says: "Spain, by its Conquistadors, was going to seek outside, by sheer energy, the strength which at home she had only potentially and which it was essential for her to realize in order to maintain her independence." Salvador de Madariaga finds in them "the typically Spanish trait: the coexistence of contrary tendencies."

[The Conquistador] is a Spaniard, the product of the conquering and mystical Spain of the sixteenth century, made in its image.

Each of these opinions, even that of Heine, who detested Spain and understood her little, has its share of the truth. Bandits at certain times—crises of panic and greed—the Conquistadors never lost their sense of grandeur. This was one of their contradictions. But the most striking was to have so closely associated the religion of self and the love of country.

The people of Spain, whatever may be her political regime, are the least possible "community-minded." They do not believe in the "collective soul," that invention of sociologists, useful sometimes as a propaganda theme but as sterile as it is theoretical. How could a collection of individuals form a single individual, at least without denying the personal soul? Deny the soul! An old proverb says that every Spaniard *"tiene su alma en su almario"*: a play on words, meaning that he keeps his soul in his closet; it is his own property, a secret thing. Pride and privation: that was the Spaniard of the sixteenth century . . .

Although fiercely individualistic, the Conquistadors were no less ardently patriotic. Every Spaniard carried in his heart a fragment of Spain and very often bathed it in his solitary tears. Andalusia had provided the first sailors, and Castile the majority of the soldiers. Columbus's sailors were almost all from Palos and Moguer, and the captains of the conquest came from Estremadura. Francisco Pizarro had recruited his companions at Trujillo, his native village; Cortés was from Medellín, Balboa from Jerez de los Caballeros, Valdivia from Villanueva de la Serena. They must have dreamed constantly of their *casa solariega* and the herd at the bottom of the field tilled by the elder brother. Manor houses with nail-studded doors, or huts of slate—the thought evokes them both. That sunburned landscape of Estremadura, with its wide and melancholy horizons, haunted the Conquistadors, and to their conquests they gave the names of home: Medellin, Guadalajara, Trujillo, Cáceres, Badajoz, and countless Santiagos. This was the compensation of these voluntary exiles, who were so attached to their homeland that one might have been able, it seems, by scratching the soles of their shoes, to find a scrap of the red clay of the Tierra de Baros.

Under the King's Eye

This Conquistador, brightly daring, taking possession of scraps of empire as he galloped along, and listening to nothing but the promptings of his own heart. . . . His plume could be seen on the narrow roads of the Andes, in the vast grasslands, by the edges of leaden lakes and upon the lava flows, and advancing by night along the rims of craters, white in the moonlight. Could nothing stop him but the fear of God? Yes, the fear of the king, for the Conquistador was not the soldier of God alone. He was the liegeman of the Spanish monarch, and his motto was that of Spain: *un monarca, un imperio, y una espada* (one monarch, one realm, and one sword). There was only one who tried to escape from royal tutelage—Gonzalo Pizarro, and he died under the executioner's ax. He who had no fear of cannibals trembled at the thought of incurring the king's wrath. Six thousand miles from Valladolid, his heart froze at the thought of displeasing Charles V. The receipt of a dispatch bearing the royal seal immediately aroused his anxiety. At a single word from the king, he did not hesitate to cross deserts, mountains, and oceans, to take orders, report, or sometimes to give himself up to justice. All, even the greatest, made this humiliating journey. Columbus (three times), Cortés, the Pizarro brothers. . . . The knee had to be bent before the Caesarian monarch if the sheet of parchment legalizing the enterprise was to be secured.

Not a caravel ever left a Spanish port in a westerly direction without a representative of the king aboard. When Columbus left for his first voyage in 1492—for the unknown, moreover—Rodrigo de Escobedo and Sánchez de

Segovia, Royal Notary and Comptroller respectively, had been forced upon him. "Master after God," the Admiral of the Ocean Sea saw the king come between himself and God. Thenceforward, the two faces could make only one. Intoxicated as they were by sudden fortune, the Conquistadors never omitted to put aside a fifth part of their booty for the royal treasury. And if any man swindled the accounts, it was at his own risk and peril: all knew that the garrote awaited the man who took it into his head to defraud the king of his share. . . .

The Romantics

"Weary of carrying their lofty miseries," "intoxicated by a heroic and brutal dream," "hoping for epic tomorrows": such was the way in which José Maria de Heredia, a Cuban descendant of the Conquistadors . . . , pictured his ancestors steering for Cipango in search of the "fabulous metal." This is the Conquistador adorned with all the romantic accessories; nothing is missing, neither violence nor insupportable pride nor the mirage of gold nor the confusion of instinct and imagination. Another feature common to the romantics was stoicism, sometimes theatrical but most often silent. Arrogant and dignified while they paced up and down the *plazuela* of their native towns, draped in their ragged capes, waiting for adventure, the Conquistadors were even more so when in the very midst of the adventure.

Romantics, indeed, with all the credulity and artless wonder that is associated with the word. Into the extravagant pact they had made with fortune the Conquistadors had brought the passionate quest for risk and the intense curiosity that always made of them something more than old campaigners. In this respect, however, they differ from the romantics, the eternally unsatisfied. The Conquistadors were overwhelmed. For once, the imagination had to admit itself surpassed by reality. No adventurer had ever known such adventure as this, and no actor had ever performed on such a stage. This splendid prize, outstretched beneath their gaze and within their reach, seemed the more beautiful to the conquerors even as the tropical sun burned into their brains. What matter? Atahualpa's treasure and the magnificence of Mexican possessions were not mirages. The enchanted forest emerged from legend to become the tangible virgin forest of America, bathed in twilight shadows.

Amadis of Gaul had turned into Pedro de Alvarado; Bernal Díaz del Castillo was about to rewrite a chivalrous novel. With eyes wide open, the Conquistadors lived in a lucid and endless delirium. . . .

Under the Pretense of Religion

"*So color de religión—van a buscar plata y oro—del encubierto tesoro . . .*" : "Under the pretense of religion, they went in search of silver and gold and of hidden treasure."

The Conquistadors used the instruments of the Faith to further their ventures.

These harsh words of Lope de Vega in his play *El Nuevo Mundo* call for comment, if not for correction. Certainly the injustices and the crimes committed in the name of religion revolt the heart as well as the conscience. Certainly the Conquistadors used the instruments of the Faith to further their ventures. Thus Ovando, when fighting in Cuba, had given the signal to an ambush by placing his hand on his cross of the Knights of Alcántara, while Valverde warned Pizarro's soldiers that the moment of attack had come by waving the Bible at Atahualpa. The system of *requerimiento* inflicted on the primitive people, the mass baptisms, the conversions *in extremis* that preceded strangulation, the expiatory stake, and the massacres that ended in the *Te Deum* seem to justify the words of one Indian, exhorted by a monk to die in the Christian faith: "Are there Spaniards in your Paradise? Then I prefer to die a heathen!" Who would dream of denying that the ceremonial of the liturgy often took on the appearance of a funeral procession? But Lope de Vega was wrong on one point: the violent acts of the Conquistadors—abduction, robberies, assassinations—though sometimes performed "in the name of" religion, were never "under the pretense of" religion.

The Conquistadors were sincere. The legality of the enterprise was guaranteed them by pontifical bulls. They had been given to understand that they were leaving for a crusade—the one against Islam having ended but recently—and that after the Jew and the Mohammedan, it was now a question of converting the Heathen. They had been born into a hatred and terror of heresy. They had wept with delight at the capture of Granada, trembled before the Inquisition, and shuddered at the very name of Luther. While still children, they had often spat at the passing of a Moor or set fire to the booth of a Jew. Spain in the sixteenth century was nothing but a vast monastery, noisy with orisons and bells. They had grown up in the shadow of cathedrals and breathed the odor of incense from their earliest years, while the first words they had uttered had been the names of the saints.

A Fanatical Spirit

The Conquistadors, although for the most part illiterate, had had no need of letters to feel the same fanatical spirit as did the horsemen of the Prophet when they invaded the old Greco-Latin world, or the Crusaders when they spread over the Syrian plains, or their own fathers at the reconquest of Granada. They had been told—they had been convinced—that millions of Indians would burn forever in Hell if they, the Conquistadors, did not bring them the Faith. They believed this quite simply. Religion was for them not a pretext

---

The Conquistadors believed in God fiercely and unreservedly. But they believed also—above all else!—in the Devil.

---

but a banner. The existence of God in three persons, the immortality of the soul, sin, the Last Judgment—it never occurred to any one of them to dispute these facts or even to discuss them. These men of war and passion had retained the faith of little children. Their confessions were sincere, they participated in the Mass not only in the flesh but also in the spirit. The worst of them died in penitence. Pierced by arrows, or with a sword blade in the throat, or tied to the stake under torture, they called loudly for the last rites. *So color de religión.* . . . What an error! No ulterior motive colored the faith of the Conquistadors. They remained men of the Middle Ages. Religious hypocrisy had not yet been invented; it was to turn up later, covering iniquity with its black cloak. The hypocrite is a creature of the seventeenth century.

The Conquistadors believed in God fiercely and unreservedly. But they believed also—above all else!—in the

Devil. Now, the New World was the empire of the Devil, a Devil with multiform face, always hideous. The somber Mexican divinities, Huitzilopochtli (the Sorcerer-Hummingbird) and Tezcatlipoca (the Smoking Mirror), the horrible Kinich Kakmo of the Mayas, the Peruvian Viracocha who symbolized boiling lava, the sinister totems of the Araucanians and Diaguites. . . . Why, the medieval demon with short horns, lustful eye, and a tail that was curled like a vine shoot seemed a "good devil" besides such as these! Spaniards who in Estremaduran twilights had taken the flight of a bat for the passing of the Evil One were naturally terrified before these monsters of stone, with bared fangs and gleaming eyes, that seemed to come to fantastic life as night fell. How could they have watched an Aztec ceremony without nausea? The black-robed priests with matted hair, burrowing with their knives in the breasts of their victims, the human skulls piled up at the feet of the teocallis, the cannibal feasts around statues spattered with putrid blood, and the charnel-house stench which all the perfumes of Mexico were never able to hide. . . .

The Prince of Darkness

Such things froze the spirits of the Conquistadors, surpassing the nightmares of their childhoods. Satan himself was there, and his worship was celebrated among the dismembered corpses. His maleficent power was honored. He was no longer, as in Spain, the familiar accomplice that could be driven off by a flick of the finger, or the shameful specter slipping furtively through one's conscience but put to flight by a sprinkling of holy water. He was enthroned. Carved in granite, incrusted with precious stones and encircled with golden serpents, he was the superb incarnation of Evil. He glorified sin. Nothing was lacking in this perfect representation of Hell, not even the pots in which certain tribes of the Colombian jungle cooked their enemies alive. This indeed was Satan himself, adorned with all his lugubrious attractions.

Why, therefore, should we be astonished at the reactions of the Spaniards? In the depths of the Indian sanctuaries they could see the Prince of Darkness standing in all his macabre splendor. Looking heavenward, they could distinguish the silvery figure of Saint James galloping across the clouds. The conflict between the true and the false, between good and evil, was manifest in this double apparition. The problem was simple and their duty was clear. The Indians were possessed of the Devil, who had to be exorcised, first by destroying the material evidence of Devil worship. This is why the conquerors, activated by the same blind zeal as early Christians when they shattered the Roman statues, overturned the pre-Columbian idols and burned the ritual articles and the manuscripts that transmitted the sacred tradition—in short, showed a holy ardor to abolish the very memory of the heathen liturgy. This they counted as pious work and a salutary need.

Why . . . should we be astonished at the reactions of the Spaniards? In the depths of the Indian sanctuaries they could see the Prince of Darkness.

Iconoclasts? Vandals? These epithets would have scandalized the Conquistadors. Who would have applied such words except the agents of Satan who served a vile master? But the Conquistadors did not limit themselves to casting down the idols. In order that the exorcism be fully effective, it was not enough to drive away the demons; it was proper also to set up in their places the symbols of the True Faith. Just as holy medals were laid upon flesh that was eaten away with ulcers, the soldiers of Charles V planted crosses on the tops of the teocallis or at crossroads. On the stones that were still spattered with blood from the sacrificial tables, they raised altars to Our Lady of Guadalupe. Tolerance was not for them. Others would follow who would use gentler methods. No one doubts that these booted and armored Christians often lacked the Christian spirit and that charity was almost always missing from their pitiless fervor; but their Faith and their good faith were whole. More even than the love of God and of one's neighbor, the horror of Beelzebub explains certain of the Conquistadors' attitudes, though of course it is understood that to explain is not to absolve.

The Conquistadors never ceased to oscillate between the opposing poles of idealism and realism. . . .

The Death of the Conquistadors

One last look at the Conquistadors. We know now how and why they lived. But how did they die? In opulence and glory? One imagines sumptuous places of retirement, or at least comfortable ones, for the captains of the conquest who had returned home with their fortunes made. They would restore the family *solar* [mansion], and those who were literate would write their memoirs. Those who were nostalgic for power would hold some honorary position at court; and as for the soldiers—those without rank—they would return to their villages in La Mancha and Estremadura. They would be rich and would buy land, and in the course of endless social gatherings they would relate their campaigns, telling the stories of the Caribbean, of treasure and princesses. They would willingly show their enormous scars, for such wounds were not to be seen every day. Think of it! Scimitars of sharpened obsidian, and darts poisoned with the juice of the manchineel tree! And they would blow out great clouds of smoke from their pipes of Mexican tobacco. . . .

The majority of the Conquistadors died while still in action, by accident, sickness, or violence.

But the reality was quite different. The majority of the Conquistadors died while still in action, by accident, sickness, or violence. Those who survived ended their days in oblivion and, some of them, in poverty. That so melancholy and wretched a fate should have distinguished these enterprises, which at the beginning had been so full of promise, seems scarcely credible. Yet examples abound, and here are some of them, chosen from the most illustrious.

First the Discoverer himself, Christopher Columbus: he died at Valladolid, cast out by the king whose glory he had made. Juan de la Cosa, the father of Atlantic pilots, died riddled with arrows. Núñez de Balboa was beheaded, on his father-in-law's orders. Díaz de Solís was stoned to death. Nicuesa was lost at sea. Ponce de León died of an arrow in the heart. Hernandez de Córdoba was mortally wounded by Indians. Hernando de Soto was carried off by fever. Pedro de Alvarado was crushed by a horse. Juan de Escalante was killed by the natives of Vera Cruz. Hernán Cortés died poor and alone in an Andalusian village. Pánfilo de Narváez was drowned. Pedro de Valdivia was devoured by cannibals. Bastidas was stabbed by one of his own lieutenants. Diego de Ordaz died of sunstroke. Pedro de Mendoza died at sea.

And what happened to the Conquistadors of Peru? Hernando Pizarro ordered Almagro garroted; the latter's son assassinated Francisco Pizarro; Vaca de Castro had the younger Almagro beheaded; and Gonzalo Pizarro, before being condemned to death by Gasca, killed Nunez de Vela. Fifty captains were hanged. Not one of those who governed Peru during a quarter of a century, except Gasca, died other than by violence.

We know now that the alliance of Spain and the New World was sealed with blood. We know, too, that those who profited greatly by the venture were not legion. Is it true, then, that wealth acquired by violence never brings happiness and that there is a curse on gold acquired unjustly? A shadow passes over the flamboyant façade of the temple of Mammon: is it the disheveled figure of the goddess Nemesis?

The drama is ended. The curtain falls slowly on a pyramid of corpses, as in the last act of a Shakespearean tragedy. It is finished, but another play is about to begin. What is its prologue?

The difficult day of the conquest has just ended in a blaze of gold and blood. *Oro y sangre*—a funereal apotheosis! Night descends upon the battlefield of the Conquistadors, and silence follows. But at dawn, into the shadows that slowly pale, phantoms slip one by one. Then day is here, and the morning light falls gradually upon these new beings, lighting their resolute features with its silver gleam. They wear neither helmet nor breastplate, but robes of monkish homespun or the sober doublets of men of law. They carry no swords, but in their hands is the mason's trowel or the ivory staff of the alcalde or the cavalier's lance. At first there are only a few, but soon a numberless crowd emerges from the shadows. They gather up the dead and bury them. The battlefield has become a cemetery. Then, in serried ranks, elbow to elbow, like the Spartan phalanxes, they move off westward. These are the colonists.

3

The Conquistadors Fought in Self-Defense

Bernal Díaz del Castillo

Bernal Díaz del Castillo, the last survivor of the Conquest of Mexico, died on his estate in Guatemala at the age of eighty-nine. He was over seventy when he began *The Conquest of New Spain*, written in part to counter errors of other historians. His first-person account is a soldier's vivid recollection, the "story of myself and my comrades, all true conquerors, who served His Majesty in the discovery, conquest, pacification, and settlement of the provinces of New Spain." In his account of the battle for Tenochtitlan, or Mexico City, the conquistador comes off as a far more vulnerable human being than is usually depicted.

Seeing that it was impossible to fill in every channel and gap that we captured in the daytime and that the Mexicans reopened and refortified each night, and that all of us together fighting, filling in, and keeping watch was very hard labour, Cortes decided to hold consultations with the captains and soldiers in his camp, and wrote to us in Alvarado's camp, and to those in Sandoval's, to learn the opinion of us all. . . .

Cortes listened to our opinions and the reasons with which we supported them. But the sole outcome of all this discussion was that next day we were to advance with all possible strength from all three camps, horsemen, crossbowmen, musketeers, and soldiers, and push forward into the great market square of Tlatelolco. When all was ready

From *The True History of the Conquest of New Spain*, by Bernal Díaz del Castillo (London: Hakluyt Society, 1908).

in the three camps, and warnings had been sent to our Tlascalan allies, the men of Texcoco, and those of the other
towns who had recently sworn obedience to His Majesty
and were to bring their canoes to help our launches, we
started from our camp on Sunday morning, after mass.
Cortes too set out from his camp, and Sandoval led his men
forward; and each company advanced in full force, capturing barricades and bridges. The Mexicans fought like brave
men, but Cortes made great gains, and so did Gonzalo de
Sandoval. As for us, we had already captured another barri-
cade and bridge, which was very difficult because Guatemoc
had great forces guarding them. Many of our men were
wounded, one so severely that he died a little later, and more
than a thousand of our Tlascalan allies were injured. Still,
we followed up our victory in high spirits.

To return to Cortes and his men, they captured a deep-
ish water-opening with a very narrow causeway across it,
which the Mexicans had constructed most cunningly. For
they had cleverly foreseen just what would happen; which
was that after his victory Cortes and his men would press
along the causeway, which would be crowded with our allies.
They decided therefore that at this point they must pretend
to be in flight, but continue to hurl javelins, arrows, and
stones and to make little stands as though trying to put up
some resistance, until they lured Cortes on to follow them.

---

*Such a furious army of shrieking, shouting, and
whistling Mexicans fell on Cortes and his men
that they could not stand up to the shock of their
charge.*

When the Mexicans saw that Cortes was indeed following up his victory in this way, they simulated flight, as they
had planned. Then, as bad fortune follows on good and great
disasters succeed great prosperity, so in his headlong pursuit
of the enemy, either out of carelessness or because Our Lord
permitted it, Cortes and his men omitted to fill in the channel they had captured. The causeway had been deliberately
built very narrow, and it was interrupted by water in some
places, and full of mud and mire. When the Mexicans saw
him cross that channel without filling it in they were highly

delighted. They had assembled great bands of warriors under very valiant captains and posted many canoes on the lake in places where our launches could not reach them on account of great stakes. All was prepared for the moment when such a furious army of shrieking, shouting, and whistling Mexicans fell on Cortes and his men that they could not stand up to the shock of their charge. Our soldiers, captains, and standard-bearers then decided to retreat in good order. But the enemy continued to charge them furiously, and drove them back to that difficult crossing. Meanwhile our allies, of whom Cortes had brought great numbers, were so confused that they turned and fled, offering no resistance. On seeing them run away in disorder Cortes tried to hearten them with cries of: 'Stop, stop, gentlemen! Stand firm! What do you mean by turning your backs?' But he could not halt them.

Mexicans Defeat Cortes

Then, at that gap in the causeway which they had neglected to fill, on that little, narrow, broken causeway, the Mexicans, aided by their canoes, defeated Cortes, wounding him in the leg, taking sixty-six of his soldiers alive, and killing eight horses. Six or seven Mexican captains had already seized our Captain, but the Lord was pleased to help him and give him strength to defend himself, although wounded. Then, in the nick of time, that very valiant soldier Cristobal de Olea came up to him and, seeing Cortes held by so many Indians, promptly killed four of them with mighty thrusts of his sword; and another brave soldier called Lerma helped him. Such was the personal bravery of these two men that the Indian captains let Cortes go. But in defending him for the second time Olea lost his life and Lerma was almost killed. Then many other soldiers rushed up and, although badly wounded, grasped Cortes and pulled him out of his dangerous position in the mud. The quartermaster Cristobal de Olid also ran forward, and they seized Cortes by the arms to drag him out of the mud and water, and brought him a horse, on which he escaped from death. At that same moment his steward Cristobal de Guzman arrived with another horse. Meanwhile the Mexican warriors went on fighting very bravely and successfully from the rooftops, inflicting great damage on us and capturing Cristobal de Guzman, whom they carried alive to Guatemoc; and they continued to pursue Cortes and his men until they had driven them back to camp. Even after that disaster, when they reached their quarters the Mexicans continued to harry them, shouting and yelling abuse and calling them cowards.

But to turn from Cortes and his defeat to our army under Pedro de Alvarado, on the causeway from Tacuba. We were advancing most victoriously when suddenly and unexpectedly we saw a great number of Mexican bands advancing against us, with handsome standards and plumes. Uttering loud yells, they threw in front of us five heads, streaming with blood, which they had just cut off the men of Cortes' company whom they had captured.

'We will kill you too,' they cried, 'as we have killed Malinche and Sandoval, and all the men they brought with them.' With these words they closed in on us, and neither cut nor thrust, nor crossbow nor musket could keep them off. They rushed at us as if we were a target. Even so, we did not break our ranks at all as we retired. We at once commanded our Tlascalan allies to get quickly out of our way in the streets and on the causeways and at the difficult places, and this time they did so with a will. When they saw those five bloodstained heads, they said that Malinche and Sandoval and all the *Teules* with them had been killed, and that the same would happen to us, and to them, the Tlascalans. They were very much frightened, for they believed what they said.

As we were retreating, we heard the sound of trumpets from the great *cue* of Huichilobos and Tezcatlipoca, which dominates the whole city, and the beating of a drum, a very sad sound as of some devilish instrument, which could be heard six miles away; and with it came the noise of many kettle-drums, conches, horns, and whistles. At that moment, as we afterwards learnt, they were offering the hearts and blood of ten of our comrades to these two idols.

At that moment, as we afterwards learnt, [the Mexicans] were offering the hearts and blood of ten of our comrades to [the] idols.

But let us return to our retreat and the great attack they made on us from the causeway, the rooftops, and the canoes on the lake. At that moment we were attacked once more by fresh bands whom Guatemoc had just sent, and he had ordered his horn to be sounded. The blowing of this horn was a signal that his captains and warriors must now fight to capture their enemies or die in the attempt, and as soon as this sound struck their ears, his bands and companies, hurling themselves on us with a terrifying and indescribable fury, endeavoured to drag us away. Even now, when I stop to think, I seem to see it all and to be present at that battle once more. It was our Lord Jesus Christ, let me repeat, who gave us strength, for we were all wounded. It was He who saved us, for otherwise we should never have reached our huts, and I praise and thank Him for it, that I escaped that time, as on other occasions, from the power of the Mexicans.

Hard Pressed and Wounded

The horsemen charged repeatedly, and with two cannon which we placed near our huts, and which were loaded and fired by turns, we managed to hold our own. The causeway was choked with Mexicans, who pursued us as far as the houses, as if we were already conquered, and hurled javelins and stones at us. But, as I have said, we killed many of them with these cannon. The most useful man that day was a gentleman called Pedro Moreno Medrano, who now lives at Puebla. He acted as gunner, because our proper artillerymen had been either killed or wounded. He was a good soldier, and gave us great assistance. While we were defending ourselves like this, hard pressed and wounded, we did not know whether Cortes and Sandoval and their armies had been killed or routed, as the Mexicans had told us when they threw down those heads, which they had brought tied together by the hair and beards. We could get no news of them, for they were fighting about a mile and a half away, and the place where the Mexicans had defeated Cortes was even further off. We were very distressed, therefore, but by keeping together in one body, both wounded and sound, we withstood the fury of the attack, which the Mexicans believed would annihilate us. For they had already captured one of our launches, killing three soldiers and wounding the captain and the rest of the crew, though it had afterwards been rescued by another launch whose captain was Juan Jaramillo; and yet another was impaled in a place from which it could not move. Its captain was Juan de Limpias, who lost his hearing at that time, and now lives at Puebla. He himself fought so valiantly, and so encouraged the soldiers who were rowing the launch, that they broke the stakes and got away, all badly wounded, thus saving the craft, which was the first to break the stakes, a great thing for us all.

Cortes and Sandoval

To return to Cortes, when he and nearly all his men were either killed or wounded, the Mexican bands made an attack on his camp, and cast in front of the soldiers who were defending it another four heads, dripping with blood, which were those of four men captured from Cortes' own army. But they said they were the heads of Tonatio—that is of Pedro de Alvarado—and of Sandoval, Bernal Díaz, and another *Teule*, and that they had already killed us all at Tacuba.

> *While we were defending ourselves . . . hard pressed and wounded, we did not know whether Cortes and Sandoval and their armies had been killed.*

It is said that Cortes was even more distressed than before, and that tears sprang to his eyes and the eyes of all those who were with him. Nevertheless he did not seem to weaken. He at once ordered Cristobal de Olid, the quartermaster, and his captains to be sure that the many Mexicans who were pressing in on them did not break into the camp, and to see that his men held together, the sound and the wounded alike. He then sent Andres de Tapia with three horsemen post-haste overland to Tacuba, to see if we were alive, and to tell us, if we had not been defeated, to keep watch by day and night, also in a single body. But we had already been doing this for some time. Tapia and his three horsemen came as hard as they could, though he and two of them were wounded, and when they reached our camp and found us fighting the Mexicans who were gathered against us, they rejoiced in their hearts. They told us how Cortes had been defeated and conveyed his message to us, but they did not care to tell us how many had been killed. They gave the number as about twenty-five, and said that the rest were well.

Sandoval and his men had advanced victoriously along the streets in the quarter they were invading. But after the defeat of Cortes, the Mexicans turned on them in such force that they could make no headway. Six soldiers were killed and all the rest injured, including Sandoval himself, who received three wounds, in the thigh, the head, and the left arm; and when the struggle was at its height, the enemy displayed six heads of Cortes' men whom they had killed, saying that these were the heads of Malinche, Tonatio, and other captains, and that Sandoval and his companions would meet with the same fate. They then made a fierce attack. When he saw the heads Sandoval told his men to show a bold spirit and not be dismayed. He warned them too that there must be no confusion on the narrow causeway as they retreated, and ordered his allies, who were numerous, to leave it immediately, since they would hamper him. Then, with the help of his two launches and his musketeers and crossbowmen, he very laboriously retired to his quarters, with all his men badly wounded and discouraged, and six of them dead. Once he was clear of the causeway, although still surrounded by Mexicans, he encouraged his people and their captains, charging them to be sure to keep together by day and night and thus prevent the camp from being overwhelmed. . . .

The Mexican bands made an attack on [Cortes's] camp, and cast in front of the soldiers . . .
another four heads, dripping with blood, which were those of four men captured from Cortes.

Just at that moment the two launches which Cortes kept under his command beside the causeway came in. There had been no news of them since the defeat. It appears that they had been caught on some stakes and, according to their captains' reports, surrounded by canoes which had attacked them. They all came in wounded, and said that in the first place God had aided them with a wind, and then by making every effort with their oars they had broken the stakes and escaped. Cortes was very pleased, for up to that time (although he had not said so in order not to dishearten the soldiers) he had given these launches up for lost, having heard nothing of them.

After this, Cortes strongly urged Sandoval to ride post-haste to our camp at Tacuba and see whether we were defeated, or how we stood; and if he found us alive, he was to help us to defend our camp from their assaults, and he instructed Francisco de Lugo to accompany him, for he knew very well that there were Mexican companies on the road. Indeed he told Lugo that he had already sent Andres de Tapia with three horsemen to get news of us, and feared they might have been killed on the way. Then, after taking his leave of him, he turned to embrace Sandoval, to whom he said: 'See, my son, I cannot go everywhere, because I am wounded. So I entrust you with the task of ensuring the safety of all three camps. I know that Pedro de Alvarado and all his comrades have fought valiantly, like true gentlemen. But I fear the great forces of these dogs may have overwhelmed them. As for me and my army, you can see our condition.'

[The Mexicans] had already driven one launch aground, killing two of its crew and wounding all the rest.

Sandoval and Francisco de Lugo rode post-haste to our position, arriving a little after dusk, and found us fighting with the Mexicans who were trying to get into our camp by way of some houses we had pulled down. Others were attacking along the causeway, and many canoes were assaulting us from the lake. They had already driven one launch aground, killing two of its crew and wounding all the rest; and Sandoval saw me with six other soldiers above our waists in the lake, helping to push it off into deep water. Many Indians were attacking us, with swords captured when Cortes was defeated or with flint-edged broadswords, trying to prevent us from rescuing the launch, which, to judge by their efforts, they intended to drag off with their canoes. Indeed, they had already attached several ropes to it in order to tow it into the city. When Sandoval saw as in this condition, he cried: 'Brothers, put your backs into it and see that they do not get the launch!' And we made such an effort that we dragged it to safety, even though, as I have said, two of its crew were killed and all the rest wounded.

Just then many companies of Mexicans came down the

causeway, wounding us all, including the horsemen. Sandoval too received a stone full in the face. But Pedro de Alvarado and some other horsemen went to his assistance. As
so many bands were coming on, and only I and twenty soldiers were opposing them, Sandoval ordered us to retire
gradually in order to save the horses; and because we did not
retire as quickly as he wished he turned on us furiously and
said: 'Do you want me and all my horsemen to be killed because of you? For my sake, Bernal Díaz, my friend, please
fall back!' Then Sandoval received another wound, and so
did his horse. By this time we had got our allies off the
causeway; and facing the enemy and never turning our
backs, we gradually retired, forming a kind of dam to hold
up their advance. Some of our crossbowmen and musketeers shot while others were loading, the horsemen made
charges, and Pedro Moreno loaded and fired his cannon.
Yet despite the number of Mexicans that were swept away
by his shot we could not keep them at bay. On the contrary,
they continued to pursue us, in the belief that they would
carry us off that night to be sacrificed.

A Terrifying Sound

When we had retired almost to our quarters, across a great
opening full of water, their arrows, darts, and stones could
no longer reach us. Sandoval, Francisco de Lugo, and Andres de Tapia were standing with Pedro de Alvarado, each
one telling his story and discussing Cortes' orders, when the
dismal drum of Huichilobos sounded again, accompanied
by conches, horns, and trumpet-like instruments. It was a
terrifying sound, and when we looked at the tall *cue* from
which it came we saw our comrades who had been captured
in Cortes' defeat being dragged up the steps to be sacrificed.
When they had hauled them up to a small platform in front
of the shrine where they kept their accursed idols we saw
them put plumes on the heads of many of them; and then
they made them dance with a sort of fan in front of
Huichilobos. Then after they had danced the papas [priests]
laid them down on their backs on some narrow stones of
sacrifice and, cutting open their chests, drew out their pal-
pitating hearts which they offered to the idols before them.
Then they kicked the bodies down the steps, and the Indian
butchers who were waiting below cut off their arms and legs
and flayed their faces, which they afterwards prepared like

glove leather, with their beards on, and kept for their drunken festivals. Then they ate their flesh with a sauce of peppers and tomatoes. They sacrificed all our men in this way, eating their legs and arms, offering their hearts and blood to their idols as I have said, and throwing their trunks and entrails to lions and tigers and serpents and snakes that they kept in the wild-beast houses I have described in an earlier chapter. On seeing these atrocities, all of us in our camp said to one another: 'Thank God they did not carry me off to be sacrificed!' My readers must remember that though we were not far off we could do nothing to help, and could only pray God to guard us from such a death. Then at the very moment of the sacrifice, great bands of Mexicans suddenly fell upon us and kept us busy on all sides. We could find no way of holding them. 'Look!' they shouted, 'that is the way you will all die, as our gods have many times promised us,' and the threats they shouted at our Tlascalan allies were so cruel and so frightening that they lost their spirit. The Mexicans threw them roasted legs of Indians and the arms of our soldiers with cries of: 'Eat the flesh of these *Teules* and of your brothers, for we are glutted with it. You can stuff yourselves on our leavings. Now see these houses you have pulled down. We shall make you build them again, much finer, with white stone and fine masonry. So go on helping the *Teules*. You will see them all sacrificed.'

They sacrificed all our men . . . eating their legs and arms, offering their hearts and entrails to lions and tigers and serpents and snakes.

Guatemoc did something more after his victory. He sent the hands and feet of our soldiers, and the skin of their faces, and the heads of the horses that had been killed, to all the towns of our allies and friends and their relations, with the message that as more than half of us were dead and he would soon finish off the rest, they had better break their alliance with us and come to Mexico, because if they did not desert us quickly he would come and destroy them.

4

The Conquistadors Fought Without Reason

Miguel Leon-Portilla

As with all conquests, that of Mexico may be written from two perspectives. While Bernal Díaz, author of the previous viewpoint, gave the point of view of the Spanish conquerors, the following selection written by Miguel Leon-Portilla gives the viewpoint of the conquered—the Aztecs.

The Aztecs believed that Cortés was Quetzalcoatl, god and culture hero who had departed to the east, promising that someday he would return from across the seas. It is thus ironic that when Cortés and his men entered Mexico, they were often welcomed not only as guests but also as gods coming home. The Aztec desire to honor the "gods" coincided with the Spanish desire for gold. Thus Motecuhzoma (Montezuma) sent out messengers with gifts. But as Cortés's forces moved toward Tenochtitlan (Mexico City), the initial "golden age" disintegrated into suspicion, manipulation, and distrust. Such distrust was often translated into brutality.

The Indians were determined to preserve their own memories of the conquest. Fray Toribio de Benevente, also known as Motolinia, arrived in June 1524 with a group of Franciscan friars. He observed the Indians' passion for history:

"Among the events of their times, the native Indians took particular note of the year in which the Spaniards entered this land, for to them it was a most remarkable happening which at first caused them great terror and amazement. They say a strange people arrive from the sea—a feat they had never before witnessed nor had known was possible—all dressed in strange garments and so bold and warlike that, although few in number, they could invade all the provinces of this land impe-

From *The Broken Spears*, by Miguel Leon-Portilla. Copyright © 1962, 1990 by Miguel Leon-Portilla. Expanded and Updated Edition © 1992 by Miguel Leon-Portilla. Reprinted by permission of Beacon Press, Boston.

riously, as if the natives were their vassals. The Indians were also filled with wonder at their horses, and the Spaniards riding on their backs. . . . They called the Spaniards 'Teteuh' meaning 'gods,' which the Spaniards corrupted into 'teules.'. . . The Indians also set down the year in which the twelve friars arrived together."

The first portion of this viewpoint was written in Nahuatl by Indian students of Fray Bernadino de Sahagun; they drew on their people's oral history, the memories of their elders who had lived through the conquest. The original version was completed about 1555. Known as the *Codex Florentino*, it was revised by Sahagun about 1585. The account of the temple massacre was gathered by Fray Diego de Duran from native sources before 1580.

Editor's Note: After the destruction of [the Mexican city of] Cholula, the Spaniards continued to march toward the Valley of Mexico, accompanied by their allies from Tlaxcala. The texts by Sahagun's informants, from which the passages in this chapter are taken, describe two incidents of particular interest.

When the army was among the volcanoes, in what the Indians called the Eagle Pass, it was met by new envoys from Motecuhzoma, headed by Tzihuacpopocatzin. The envoys presented many objects of gold to the strangers, and then observed their reactions to the gifts: "The Spaniards burst into smiles. . . . They hungered like pigs for that gold. . . ."

Second, the texts report the deceit of Tzihuacpopocatzin, who attempted—apparently on Motecuhzoma's order—to pass himself off as Motecuhzoma. This effort failed, and another series of envoys was sent out—magicians again—in the hope of stopping the conquistadors. But the wizards retired before the mysterious presence of a pretended drunkard, who foretold the ruin of Mexico and showed them portents. They thought the god Tezcatlipoca had appeared to them, and they hurried back to Tenochtitlan to tell Motecuhzoma. The great Aztec *tlatoani* was even more depressed than before and waited fatalistically for what was to come.

The Spaniards See the Objects of Gold

Then Motecuhzoma dispatched various chiefs. Tzi-huacpopocatzin was at their head, and he took with him a great many of his representatives. They went out to meet the Spaniards in the vicinity of Popocatepetl and Iztactepetl, there in the Eagle Pass.

They gave the "gods" ensigns of gold, and ensigns of quetzal feathers, and golden necklaces. And when they were given these presents, the Spaniards burst into smiles; their eyes shone with pleasure; they were delighted by them. They picked up the gold and fingered it like monkeys; they seemed to be transported by joy, as if their hearts were illumined and made new.

[The Conquistadors] longed and lusted for gold. Their bodies swelled with greed, and their hunger was ravenous, they hungered like pigs for that gold.

The truth is that they longed and lusted for gold. Their bodies swelled with greed, and their hunger was ravenous, they hungered like pigs for that gold. They snatched at the golden ensigns, waved them from side to side and examined every inch of them. They were like one who speaks a barbarous tongue: everything they said was in a barbarous tongue. . . .

Speeches of Motecuhzoma and Cortes

When Motecuhzoma had given necklaces to each one, Cortes asked him: "Are you Motecuhzoma? Are you the king? Is it true that you are the king Motecuhzoma?"

And the king said: "Yes, I am Motecuhzoma." Then he stood up to welcome Cortes; he came forward, bowed his head low and addressed him in these words: "Our lord, you are weary. The journey has tired you, but now you have arrived on the earth. You have come to your city, Mexico. You have come here to sit on your throne, to sit under its canopy.

"The kings who have gone before, your representatives, guarded it and preserved it for your coming. The kings Itzcoatl, Motecuhzoma the Elder, Axayacatl, Tizoc and Ahuitzol ruled for you in the City of Mexico. The people were protected by their swords and sheltered by their shields.

"Do the kings know the destiny of those they left behind, their posterity? If only they are watching! If only they can see what I see!

"No, it is not a dream. I am not walking in my sleep. I am not seeing you in my dreams. . . . I have seen you at last! I have met you face to face! I was in agony for five days, for ten days, with my eyes fixed on the Region of the Mystery. And now you have come out of the clouds and mists to sit on your throne again.

"This was foretold by the kings who governed your city, and now it has taken place. You have come back to us; you have come down from the sky. Rest now, and take possession of your royal houses. Welcome to your land, my lords!"

Nothing to Fear from Friends

When Motecuhzoma had finished, La Malinche translated his address into Spanish so that the Captain could understand it. Cortes replied in his strange and savage tongue, speaking first to La Malinche: "Tell Motecuhzoma that we are his friends. There is nothing to fear. We have wanted to see him for a long time, and now we have seen his face and heard his words. Tell him that we love him well and that our hearts are contented."

Then he said to Motecuhzoma: "We have come to your house in Mexico as friends. There is nothing to fear."

La Malinche translated this speech and the Spaniards grasped Motecuhzoma's hands and patted his back to show their affection for him.

The Spaniards examined everything they saw. They dismounted from their horses, and mounted them again, and dismounted again, so as not to miss anything of interest.

The chiefs who accompanied Motecuhzoma were: Cacama, king of Tezcoco; Tetlepanquetzaltzin, king of Tlacopan; Itzcuauhtzin the Tlacochcalcatl, lord of Tlatelolco; and Topantemoc, Motecuhzoma's treasurer in Tlatelolco. These four chiefs were standing in a file.

The other princes were: Atlixcatzin [chief who has taken captives]; Tepeoatzin, the Tlacochcalcatl; Quetzalaztatzin, the keeper of the chalk; Totomotzin; Hecateu-patilzin; and Cuappiatzin.

When Motecuhzoma was imprisoned, they all went into hiding. They ran away to hide and treacherously abandoned him!

The Spaniards Take Possession of the City

When the Spaniards entered the Royal House, they placed Motecuhzoma under guard and kept him under their vigilance. They also placed a guard over Itzcuauhtzin, but the other lords were permitted to depart.

Then the Spaniards fired one of their cannons, and this caused great confusion in the city. The people scattered in every direction; they fled without rhyme or reason; they ran off as if they were being pursued. It was as if they had eaten the mushrooms that confuse the mind, or had seen some dreadful apparition. They were all overcome by terror, as if their hearts had fainted. And when night fell, the panic spread through the city and their fears would not let them sleep.

[The Mexicans] were all overcome by terror . . . and when night fell, the panic spread through the city.

In the morning the Spaniards told Motecuhzoma what they needed in the way of supplies: tortillas, fried chickens, hens' eggs, pure water, firewood and charcoal. Also: large, clean cooking pots, water jars, pitchers, dishes and other pottery. Motecuhzoma ordered that it be sent to them. The chiefs who received this order were angry with the king and no longer revered or respected him. But they furnished the Spaniards with all the provisions they needed— food, beverages and water, and fodder for the horses.

The Spaniards Reveal Their Greed

When the Spaniards were installed in the palace, they asked Motecuhzoma about the city's resources and reserves and about the warriors' ensigns and shields. They questioned him closely and then demanded gold.

Motecuhzoma guided them to it. They surrounded him and crowded close with their weapons. He walked in the center, while they formed a circle around him.

When they arrived at the treasure house called Teu-calco, the riches of gold and feathers were brought out to them: ornaments made of quetzal feathers, richly worked shields, disks of gold, the necklaces of the idols, gold nose plugs, gold greaves and bracelets and crowns.

The Spaniards searched through the whole treasure house, questioning and quarreling, and seized every object they thought was beautiful.

The Spaniards immediately stripped the feathers from the gold shields and ensigns. They gathered all the gold into a great mound and set fire to everything else, regard-less of its value. Then they melted down the gold into in-gots. As for the precious green stones, they took only the best of them; the rest were snatched up by the Tlaxcalte-cas. The Spaniards searched through the whole treasure house, questioning and quarreling, and seized every object they thought was beautiful.

The Seizure of Motecuhzoma's Treasures

Next they went to Motecuhzoma's storehouse, in the place called Totocalco [Place of the Palace of the Birds], where his personal treasures were kept. The Spaniards grinned like little beasts and patted each other with delight.

When they entered the hall of treasures, it was as if they had arrived in Paradise. They searched everywhere and coveted everything; they were slaves to their own greed. All of Motecuhzoma's possessions were brought out: fine bracelets, necklaces with large stones, ankle rings with little gold bells, the royal crowns and all the royal finery—everything that belonged to the king and was re-served to him only. They seized these treasures as if they were their own, as if this plunder were merely a stroke of good luck. And when they had taken all the gold, they heaped up everything else in the middle of the patio.

La Malinche called the nobles together. She climbed up to the palace roof and cried: "Mexicanos, come for-ward! The Spaniards need your help! Bring them food and pure water. They are tired and hungry; they are almost fainting from exhaustion! Why do you not come forward? Are you angry with them?"

The Mexicans were too frightened to approach. They were crushed by terror and would not risk coming forward. They shied away as if the Spaniards were wild beasts, as if the hour were midnight on the blackest night of the year. Yet they did not abandon the Spaniards to hunger and thirst. They brought them whatever they needed, but shook with fear as they did so. They delivered the supplies to the Spaniards with trembling hands, then turned and hurried away. . . .

[The Mexicans] did not abandon the Spaniards to hunger and thirst. They brought them whatever they needed, but shook with fear as they did so.

Editor's Note: Several indigenous texts—the Codex Ramirez, *the* XIII *relación of Alva Ixtlilxochitl and the* Codex Aubin—*describe the massacre perpetrated during the fiesta of Toxcatl, which the Aztecs celebrated in honor of the god Huitzilopochtli. "This was the most important of their fiestas,"* wrote Sahagun. *"It was like our Easter and fell at almost the same time."*

Cortes had been absent from the city for twenty days when the massacre took place; he had gone out to fight Panfilo de Narvaez, who was coming to arrest him by order of Diego Velazques, governor of Cuba. Cortes' deputy, Pedro de Alvarado, treacherously murdered the celebrants when the festival was at its height.

The Aztecs begged permission of their king to hold the fiesta of Huitzilopochtli. The Spaniards wanted to see this fiesta to learn how it was celebrated. A delegation of the celebrants came to the palace where Motecuhzoma was a prisoner, and when their spokesman asked his permission, he granted it to them.

As soon as the delegation returned, the women began to grind seeds of the chicalote. These women had fasted for a whole year. They ground the seeds in the patio of the temple.

The Spaniards came out of the palace together, dressed in armor and carrying their weapons with them.

They stalked among the women and looked at them one by one; they stared into the faces of the women who were grinding seeds. After this cold inspection, they went back into the palace. It is said that they planned to kill the celebrants if the men entered the patio.

[The Conquistadors] stalked among the women and looked at them one by one; they stared into the faces of the women.

The Statue of Huitzilopochtli, the God of War

On the evening before the fiesta of Toxcatl, the celebrants began to model a statue of Huitzilopochtli. They gave it such a human appearance that it seemed the body of a living man. Yet they made the statue with nothing but a paste made of the ground seeds of the chicalote, which they shaped over an armature of sticks.

When the statue was finished, they dressed it in rich feathers, and they painted crossbars over and under its eyes. They also clipped on its earrings of turquoise mosaic; these were in the shape of serpents, with gold rings hanging from them. Its nose plug, in the shape of an arrow, was made of gold and was inlaid with fine stones.

They placed the magic headdress of hummingbird feathers on its head. They also adorned it with an *anecuyotl*, which was a belt made of feathers, with a cone at the back. Then they hung around its neck an ornament of yellow parrot feathers, fringed like the locks of a young boy. Over this they put its nettle-leaf cape, which was painted black and decorated with five clusters of eagle feathers.

Next they wrapped it in its cloak, which was painted with skulls and bones, and over this they fastened its vest. The vest was painted with dismembered human parts: skulls, ears, hearts, intestines, torsos, breasts, hands and feet. They also put on its *maxtlatl*, or loincloth, which was decorated with images of dissevered limbs and fringed with amate paper [made from inner bark of several trees of the genus *Ficus*]. This *maxtlatl* was painted with vertical stripes of bright blue.

They fastened a red paper flag at its shoulder and placed on its head what looked like a sacrificial flint knife.

This too was made of red paper; it seemed to have been steeped in blood.

The statue carried a *tehuehuelli*, a bamboo shield decorated with four clusters of fine eagle feathers. The pendant of this shield was blood-red, like the knife and the shoulder flag. The statue also carried four arrows.

Finally, they put the wristbands on its arms. These bands, made of coyote skin, were fringed with paper cut into little strips.

Early the next morning, the statue's face was uncovered by those who had been chosen for that ceremony. They gathered in front of the idol in single file and offered it gifts of food, such as round seedcakes or perhaps human flesh. But they did not carry it up to its temple on top of the pyramid.

All the young warriors were eager for the fiesta to begin. They had sworn to dance and sing with all their hearts, so that the Spaniards would marvel at the beauty of the rituals.

The procession began, and the celebrants filed into the temple patio to dance the Dance of the Serpent. When they were all together in the patio, the songs and the dance began. Those who had fasted for twenty days and those who had fasted for a year were in command of the others; they kept the dancers in file with their pine wands. (If anyone wished to urinate, he did not stop dancing, but simply opened his clothing at the hips and separated his clusters of heron feathers.)

If anyone disobeyed the leaders or was not in his proper place they struck him on the hips and shoulders. Then they drove him out of the patio, beating him and shoving him from behind. They pushed him so hard that he sprawled to the ground, and they dragged him outside by the ears. No one dared to say a word about this punishment, for those who had fasted during the year were feared and venerated; they had earned the exclusive title "Brothers of Huitzilopochtli."

The great captains, the bravest warriors, danced at the head of the files to guide the others. The youths followed at a slight distance. Some of the youths wore their hair gathered into large locks, a sign that they had never taken any captives. Others carried their headdresses on their shoulders; they had taken captives, but only with help.

Then came the recruits, who were called "the young warriors." They had each captured an enemy or two. The others called to them: "Come, comrades, show us how brave you are! Dance with all your hearts!"

The Spaniards Attack the Celebrants

At this moment in the fiesta, when the dance was loveliest and when song was linked to song, the Spaniards were seized with an urge to kill the celebrants. They all ran forward, armed as if for battle. They closed the entrances and passageways, all the gates of the patio: the Eagle Gate in the lesser palace, the Gate of the Canestalk and the Gate of the Serpent of Mirrors. They posted guards so that no one could escape, and then rushed into the Sacred Patio to slaughter the celebrants. They came on foot, carrying their swords and their wooden or metal shields.

At this moment in the fiesta, when the dance was loveliest . . . the Spaniards were seized with an urge to kill the celebrants.

They ran in among the dancers, forcing their way to the place where the drums were played. They attacked the man who was drumming and cut off his arms. Then they cut off his head, and it rolled across the floor.

They attacked all the celebrants, stabbing them, spearing them, striking them with their swords. They attacked some of them from behind, and these fell instantly to the ground with their entrails hanging out. Others they beheaded: they cut off their heads, or split their heads to pieces.

They struck others in the shoulders, and their arms were torn from their bodies. They wounded some in the thigh and some in the calf. They slashed others in the abdomen, and their entrails all spilled to the ground. Some attempted to run away, but their intestines dragged as they ran; they seemed to tangle their feet in their own entrails. No matter how they tried to save themselves, they could find no escape.

Some attempted to force their way out, but the Spaniards murdered them at the gates. Others climbed the walls, but they could not save themselves. Those who ran into the communal houses were safe there for a while; so were those who lay down among the victims and pretended to be dead. But if they stood up again, the Spaniards saw them and killed them.

The blood of the warriors flowed like water and gathered into pools. The pools widened, and the stench of blood and entrails filled the air. The Spaniards ran into the communal houses to kill those who were hiding. They ran everywhere and searched everywhere; they invaded every room, hunting and killing.

When the news of this massacre was heard outside the Sacred Patio, a great cry went up: "Mexicanos, come running! Bring your spears and shields! The strangers have murdered our warriors!"

They attacked the celebrants, stabbing them, spearing them, striking them with their swords.

This cry was answered with a roar of grief and anger: the people shouted and wailed and beat their palms against their mouths. The captains assembled at once, as if the hour had been determined in advance. They all carried their spears and shields.

Then the battle began. The Aztecs attacked with javelins and arrows, even with the light spears that are used for hunting birds. They hurled their javelins with all their strength, and the cloud of missiles spread out over the Spaniards like a yellow cloak.

The Spaniards immediately took refuge in the palace. They began to shoot at the Mexicans with their iron arrows and to fire their cannons and arquebuses. And they shackled Motecuhzoma in chains.

The Mexicans who had died in the massacre were taken out of the patio one by one and inquiries were made to discover their names. The fathers and mothers of the dead wept and lamented.

Each victim was taken first to his own home and then to the Sacred Patio, where all the dead were brought together. Some of the bodies were later burned in the place called the Eagle Urn, and others in the House of the Young Men.

Chapter 3

The Indians

1

White Takeover of Indian Land: A White's View

Theodore Roosevelt

Theodore Roosevelt, the twenty-sixth president of the United States, was born in 1858. Having attended Columbia Law School after graduation from Harvard in 1880, he was well on his way toward a successful and satisfying personal and professional life. Married, by age twenty-four the author of *The Naval War of 1812*, recently elected to the New York legislature, Roosevelt seemed to have it all. Then, on February 14, 1884, two days after the birth of his first child, Roosevelt lost both his mother and his wife within a few hours. Stunned, he dropped out of politics, left his baby daughter with his sister, and went west to the North Dakota ranch which he had bought the previous year. He stayed there for two years, recovering his health and developing from a somewhat frail asthmatic to a robust outdoorsman as he actively participated in the daily life of the ranch. Roosevelt derived *Hunting Trips of a Ranchman* (1885), *Ranch Life and the Hunting Trail* (1888) and *The Wilderness Hunter* (1893) from this experience. In 1886 he returned to the east, was offered the Republican nomination for the mayor of New York City, lost the election, left for Europe and married. Returning to the United States early in 1887, he planned to write a grandiose history of European exploration and settlement of North America. The first two volumes of this work, *The Winning of the West*, were published in 1889. The following viewpoint is excerpted from the first volume of that work.

From *The Winning of the West*, vol. 1, by Theodore Roosevelt (New York: Putnam, 1903).

Border warfare . . . was a war waged by savages against armed settlers, whose families followed them into the wilderness. Such a war is inevitably bloody and cruel; but the inhuman love of cruelty for cruelty's sake, which marks the red Indian above all other savages, rendered these wars more terrible than any others. For the hideous, unnamable, unthinkable tortures practised by the red men on their captured foes, and on their foes' tender women and helpless children, were such as we read of in no other struggle, hardly even in the revolting pages that tell the deeds of the Holy Inquisition. It was inevitable—indeed it was in many instances proper—that such deeds should awake in the breasts of the whites the grimmest, wildest spirit of revenge and hatred.

The inhuman love of cruelty for cruelty's sake, which marks the red Indian above all other savages, rendered these [border] wars more terrible than any others.

The history of the border wars, both in the ways they were begun and in the ways they were waged, makes a long tale of injuries inflicted, suffered, and mercilessly revenged. It could not be otherwise when brutal, reckless, lawless borderers, despising all men not of their own color, were thrown in contact with savages who esteemed cruelty and treachery as the highest of virtues, and rapine and murder as the worthiest of pursuits. Moreover, it was sadly inevitable that the law-abiding borderer as well as the white ruffian, the peaceful Indian as well as the painted marauder, should be plunged into the struggle to suffer the punishment that should only have fallen on their evil-minded fellows.

Looking back, it is easy to say that much of the wrongdoing could have been prevented; but if we examine the facts to find out the truth, not to establish a theory, we are bound to admit that the struggle was really one that could not possibly have been avoided. The sentimental historians speak as if the blame had been all ours, and the wrong all done to our foes, and as if it would have been possible by any exercise of wisdom to reconcile claims that were in their very essence conflicting; but their utterances are as shallow as they are untruthful. Unless we were willing that the whole continent west of the Alleghanies should remain an unpeopled waste, the hunting-ground of savages, war was inevitable; and even had we been willing, and had we refrained from encroaching on the Indians' lands, the war would have come nevertheless, for then the Indians themselves would have encroached on ours. Undoubtedly we have wronged many tribes; but equally undoubtedly our first definite knowledge of many others has been derived from their unprovoked outrages upon our people. The Chippewas, Ottawas, and Pottawatamies furnished hundreds of young warriors to the parties that devastated our frontiers generations before we in any way encroached upon or wronged them.

Land Hunger a Cause for War

Mere outrages could be atoned for or settled; the question which lay at the root of our difficulties was that of the occupation of the land itself, and to this there could be no solution save war. The Indians had no ownership of the land in the way in which we understand the term. The tribes lived far apart; each had for its hunting-grounds all the territory from which it was not barred by rivals. Each looked with jealousy upon all interlopers, but each was prompt to act as an interloper when occasion offered. Every good hunting-ground was claimed by many nations. It was rare, indeed, that any tribe had an uncontested title to a large tract of land; where such title existed, it rested, not on actual occupancy and cultivation, but on the recent butchery of weaker rivals. For instance, there were a dozen tribes, all of whom hunted in Kentucky, and fought each other there, all of whom had equally good titles to the soil, and not one of whom acknowledged the right of any other; as a matter of fact they had therein no right, save the right of the strongest. The land no more belonged to them than it belonged to Boon and the white hunters who first visited it.

The Indians had no ownership of the land in the way in which we understand the term.

On the borders there are perpetual complaints of the encroachments of whites upon Indian lands; and naturally the central government at Washington, and before it was at

Washington, has usually been inclined to sympathize with the feeling that considers the whites the aggressors, for the government does not wish a war, does not itself feel any land hunger, hears of not a tenth of the Indian outrages, and knows by experience that the white borderers are not easy to rule. As a consequence, the official reports of the people who are not on the ground are apt to paint the Indian side in its most favorable light, and are often completely untrustworthy, this being particularly the case if the author of the report is an eastern man, utterly unacquainted with the actual condition of affairs on the frontier.

Indians Have No True Title to the Land

Such a man, though both honest and intelligent, when he hears that the whites have settled on Indian lands, cannot realize that the act has no resemblance whatever to the forcible occupation of land already cultivated. The white settler has merely moved into an uninhabited waste; he does not feel that he is committing a wrong, for he knows perfectly well that the land is really owned by no one. It is never even visited, except perhaps for a week or two every year, and then the visitors are likely at any moment to be driven off by a rival hunting-party of greater strength. The settler ousts no one from the land; if he did not chop down the trees, hew out the logs for a building, and clear the ground for tillage, no one else would do so. He drives out the game, however, and of course the Indians who live thereon sink their mutual animosities and turn against the intruder. The truth is, the Indians never had any real title to the soil; they had not half as good a claim to it, for instance, as the cattlemen now have to all eastern Montana, yet no one would assert that the cattlemen have a right to keep immigrants off their vast unfenced ranges. The settler and pioneer have at bottom had justice on their side; this great continent could not have been kept as nothing but a game preserve for squalid savages. Moreover, to the most oppressed Indian nations the whites often acted as a protection, or, at least, they deferred instead of hastening their fate. But for the interposition of the whites it is probable that the Iroquois would have exterminated every Algonquin tribe before the end of the eighteenth century; exactly as in recent time the Crows and Pawnees would have been destroyed by the Sioux, had it not been for the wars we have waged against the latter.

Again, the loose governmental system of the Indians made it as difficult to secure a permanent peace with them as it was to negotiate the purchase of the lands. The sachem, or hereditary peace chief, and the elective war chief, who wielded only the influence that he could secure by his personal prowess and his tact, were equally unable to control all of their tribesmen, and were powerless with their confederated nations. If peace was made with the Shawnees, the war was continued by the Miamis; if peace was made with the latter, nevertheless perhaps one small band was dissatisfied, and continued the contest on its own account; and even if all the recognized bands were dealt with, the parties of renegades or outlaws had to be considered; and in the last resort the full recognition accorded by the Indians to the right of private warfare, made it possible for any individual warrior who possessed any influence to go on raiding and murdering unchecked. Every tribe, every sub-tribe, every band of a dozen souls ruled over by a petty chief, almost every individual warrior of the least importance, had to be met and pacified. Even if peace were declared, the Indians could not exist long without breaking it. There was to them no temptation to trespass on the white man's ground for the purpose of settling; but every young brave was brought up to regard scalps taken and horses stolen, in war or peace, as the highest proofs and tokens of skill and courage, the sure means of attaining glory and honor, the admiration of men and the love of women. Where the young men thought thus, and the chiefs had so little real control, it was inevitable that there should be many unprovoked forays for scalps, slaves, and horses made upon the white borderers.

The settler and pioneer have at bottom had justice on their side; this great continent could not have been kept as nothing but a game preserve for squalid savages.

As for the whites themselves, they too have many and grievous sins against their red neighbors for which to answer. They cannot be severely blamed for trespassing upon what was called the Indian's land; for let sentimentalists say what they will, the man who puts the soil to use must of right dispossess the man who does not, or the world will come to a standstill; but for many of their other deeds there can be no pardon. On the border each man was a law unto himself, and good and bad alike were left in perfect freedom to follow out to the uttermost limits their own desires; for the spirit of individualism so characteristic of American life reached its extreme of development in the backwoods. The whites who wished peace, the magistrates and leaders, had little more power over their evil and unruly fellows than the Indian sachems had over the turbulent young braves. Each man did what seemed best in his own eyes, almost without let or hindrance; unless, indeed, he trespassed upon the rights of his neighbors, who were ready enough to band together in their own defence, though slow to interfere in the affairs of others.

Misdeeds of the Borderers

Thus the men of lawless, brutal spirit who are found in every community and who flock to places where the reign of order is lax, were able to follow the bent of their inclinations unchecked. They utterly despised the red man; they held it no crime whatever to cheat him in trading, to rob him of his peltries or horses, to murder him if the fit seized them. Criminals who generally preyed on their own neighbors, found it easier, and perhaps hardly as dangerous, to pursue their calling at the expense of the redskins, for the latter, when they discovered that they had been wronged, were quite as apt to vent their wrath on some outsider as on the original offender. If they injured a white, all the whites might make common cause against them; but if they injured a red man, though there were sure to be plenty of whites who disapproved of it, there were apt to be very few indeed whose disapproval took any active shape.

Each race stood by its own members, and each held all of the other race responsible for the misdeeds of a few uncontrollable spirits; and this clannishness among those of one color, and the refusal or the inability to discriminate between the good and the bad of the other color were the two most fruitful causes of border strife. When, even if he sought to prevent them, the innocent man was sure to suffer for the misdeeds of the guilty, unless both joined together for defence, the former had no alternative save to make common cause with the latter. Moreover, in a sparse backwoods settlement, where the presence of a strong, vigorous fighter was a source of safety to the whole community, it was impossible to expect that he would be punished with severity for offences which, in their hearts, his fellow townsmen could not help regarding as in some sort a revenge for the injuries they had themselves suffered. Every quiet, peaceable settler had either himself been grievously wronged, or had been an eye-witness to wrongs done to his friends; and while these were vivid in his mind, the corresponding wrongs done the Indians were never brought home to him at all. If his son was scalped or his cattle driven off, he could not be expected to remember that perhaps the Indians who did the deed had themselves been cheated by a white trader, or had lost a relative at the hands of some border ruffian, or felt aggrieved because a hundred miles off some settler had built a cabin on lands they considered their own. When he joined with other exasperated and injured men to make a retaliatory inroad, his vengeance might or might not fall on the heads of the real offenders; and, in any case, he was often not in the frame of mind to put a stop to the outrages sure to be committed by the brutal spirits among his allies—though these brutal spirits were probably in a small minority.

Every quiet, peaceable settler had either himself been grievously wronged, or had been an eye-witness to wrongs done to his friends.

Avenging Wrongs

The excesses so often committed by the whites, when, after many checks and failures, they at last grasped victory, are causes for shame and regret; yet it is only fair to keep in mind the terrible provocations they had endured. Mercy, pity, magnanimity to the fallen, could not be expected from the frontiersmen gathered together to war against an Indian tribe. Almost every man of such a band had bitter personal wrongs to avenge. He was not taking part in a war against a civilized foe; he was fighting in a contest where women and children suffered the fate of the strong men, and instead of enthusiasm for his country's flag and a general national animosity towards its enemies, he was actuated by a furious flame of hot anger, and was goaded on by memories of which merely to think was madness. His friends had been treacherously slain while on messages of peace; his house had been burned, his cattle driven off, and all he had in the world destroyed before he knew that war existed and when he felt quite guiltless of all offence; his sweetheart or wife had been carried off, ravished, and was at the moment the slave and concubine of some dirty and brutal Indian warrior; his son, the stay of house, had been burned at the stake with torments too horrible to mention; his sister, when ransomed and returned to him, had told of the weary journey through the woods, when she carried around her neck as a horrible necklace the bloody scalps of her husband and children; seared into his eyeballs, into his very brain, he bore ever with him, waking or sleeping, the sight of the skinned, mutilated, hideous body of the baby who had just grown old enough to recognize him and to crow and laugh when taken in his arms. Such incidents as these were not exceptional; one or more, and often all of them, were the invariable attendants of every one of the countless Indian inroads that took place during the long generations of forest warfare. It was small wonder that men who had thus lost every thing should sometimes be fairly crazed by their wrongs. Again and again on the frontier we hear of some such unfortunate who has devoted all the remainder of his wretched life to the one object of taking vengeance on the whole race of the men who had darkened his days forever. Too often the squaws and pappooses fell victims of the vengeance that should have come only on the warriors; for the whites regarded their foes as beasts rather than men, and knew that the squaws were more cruel than others in torturing the prisoner, and that the very children took their full part therein, being held up by their fathers to tomahawk the dying victims at the stake.

Thus it is that there are so many dark and bloody pages in the book of border warfare, that grim and iron-bound volume, wherein we read how our forefathers won the wide lands that we inherit. It contains many a tale of fierce heroism and adventurous ambition, of the daring and resolute courage of men and the patient endurance of women; it shows us a stem race of freemen who toiled hard, endured greatly, and fronted adversity bravely, who prized strength and courage and good faith, whose wives were chaste, who were generous and loyal to their friends. But it shows us also how they spurned at restraint and fretted under it, how they would brook no wrong to themselves, and yet too often inflicted wrong on others; their feats of terrible prowess are interspersed with deeds of the foulest and most wanton aggression, the darkest treachery, the most revolting cruelty; and though we meet with plenty of the rough, strong, coarse virtues, we see but little of such qualities as mercy for the fallen, the weak, and the helpless, or pity for a gallant and vanquished foe.

2

White Takeover of Indian Land: An Indian's View

Chief Joseph

In June 1877, only a year after Custer's defeat, an unexpected Indian outbreak occurred. The Nez Percé had for centuries centered their settlements on the territory where Washington, Oregon, and Idaho meet. With their horses, however, they traveled great distances to northern Idaho and Washington, to the Pacific and the mouth of the Columbia, and across the Bitterroots to the Plains for hunting, war, or trade. Their relations with the whites had always been peaceful. They welcomed Lewis and Clark in 1805; Canadian fur traders with the North West Company provided them with guns and their name, from the pieces of shell some wore in their noses; and in the 1820s some young were taken to an Anglican mission school in central Canada and, returning, stirred an interest in Christianity among tribespeople. The Reverend Spaulding, to whom Joseph refers, started a Presbyterian mission at Lapwai in 1836. Eventually, however, many Nez Percés became disillusioned with the white man's religion. When settlers began to pour into Oregon in the 1840s, many Indians thought the Spauldings had conspired to steal their country. Concerned at these suspicions and frightened by the news that the Marcus Whitmans, missionaries to the nearby Cayuse Indians, had been massacred, the Spauldings fled. The Nez Percés' suspicions that the whites were out to steal their land received confirmation when gold was found in 1860 and miners and prospectors poured in. More settlers followed. In 1863 an agreement was signed between government commissioners and some bands of the Nez Percé,

From "An Indian's View of Indian Affairs," by Chief Joseph, *North American Review*, April 1879.

ceding three quarters of their land, including the Wallowa Valley, to the whites. Chief Joseph's band was not among those present at the signing. His account of the conflict, excerpted here, was published in the April 1879 issue of *North American Review*.

M̶y friends, I have been asked to show you my heart. I am glad to have a chance to do so. I want the white people to understand my people. Some of you think an Indian is like a wild animal. This is a great mistake. I will tell you all about our people, and then you can judge whether an Indian is a man or not. I believe much trouble and blood would be saved if we opened our hearts more. I will tell you in my way how the Indian sees things. The white man has more words to tell you how they look to him, but it does not require many words to speak the truth. What I have to say will come from my heart, and I will speak with a straight tongue. Ah-cum-kin-i-ma-me-hut (the Great Spirit) is looking at me, and will hear me.

> *Some of you think an Indian is like a wild animal. This is a great mistake.*

My name is In-mut-too-yah-lat-lat (Thunder traveling over the Mountains). I am chief of the Wal-lam-wat-kin band of Chute-pa-1u, or Nez Percés (nose-pierced Indians). I was born in eastern Oregon, thirty-eight winters ago. My father was chief before me. When a young man, he was called Joseph by Mr. Spaulding, a missionary. He died a few years ago. There was no stain on his hands of the blood of a white man. He left a good name on the earth. He advised me well for my people.

Our fathers gave us many laws, which they had learned from their fathers. These laws were good. They told us to treat all men as they treated us; that we should never be the first to break a bargain; that it was a disgrace to tell a lie; that we should speak only the truth; that it was a shame for one man to take from another his wife, or his property without paying for it. We were taught to believe that the Great Spirit sees and hears everything, and that he never forgets;

that hereafter he will give every man a spirit-home according to his deserts: if he has been a good man, he will have a good home; if he has been a bad man, he will have a bad home. This I believe, and all my people believe the same.

We Met the First White Men

We did not know there were other people besides the Indian until about one hundred winters ago, when some men with white faces came to our country. They brought many things with them to trade for furs and skins. They brought tobacco, which was new to us. They brought guns with flint stones on them, which frightened our women and children. Our people could not talk with these white-faced men, but they used signs which all people understand. These men were Frenchmen, and they called our people "Nez Percés," because they wore rings in their noses for ornaments. Although very few of our people wear them now, we are still called by the same name. These French trappers said a great many things to our fathers, which have been planted in our hearts. Some were good for us, but some were bad. Our people were divided in opinion about these men. Some thought they taught more bad than good. An Indian respects a brave man, but he despises a coward. He loves a straight tongue, but he hates a forked tongue. The French trappers told us some truths and some lies.

We soon found that the white men were growing rich very fast, and were greedy to possess everything the Indian had.

The first white men of your people who came to our country were named Lewis and Clarke [*sic*]. They also brought many things that our people had never seen. They talked straight, and our people gave them a great feast, as a proof that their hearts were friendly. These men were very kind. They made presents to our chiefs and our people made presents to them. We had a great many horses, of which we gave them what they needed, and they gave us guns and tobacco in return. All the Nez Percés made friends with Lewis and Clarke, and agreed to let them pass through their country, and never to make war on white men. This promise the Nez Percés have never broken. No white man can accuse them of bad faith, and speak with a straight tongue. It has always been the pride of the Nez Percés that they were the friends of the white men. When my father was a young man there came to our country a white man (Rev. Mr. Spaulding) who talked spirit law. He won the affections of our people because he spoke good things to them. At first he did not say anything about white men wanting to settle on our lands. Nothing was said about that until about twenty winters ago, when a number of white people came into our country and built houses and made farms. At first our people made no complaint. They thought there was room enough for all to live in peace, and they were learning many things from the white men that seemed to be good. But we soon found that the white men were growing rich very fast, and were greedy to possess everything the Indian had. My father was the first to see through the schemes of the white men, and he warned his tribe to be careful about trading with them. He had suspicion of men who seemed so anxious to make money. I was a boy then, but I remember well my father's caution. He had sharper eyes than the rest of our people.

My Father Wished to Be a Free Man

Next there came a white officer (Governor Stevens), who invited all the Nez Percés to a treaty council. After the council was opened he made known his heart. He said there were a great many white people in the country, and many more would come, that he wanted the land marked out so that the Indians and white men could be separated. If they were to live in peace it was necessary, he said, that the Indians should have a country set apart for them, and in that country they must stay. My father, who represented his band, refused to have anything to do with the council, because he wished to be a free man. He claimed that no man owned any part of the earth, and a man could not sell what he did not own.

Mr. Spaulding took hold of my father's arm and said, "Come and sign the treaty." My father pushed him away, and said: "Why do you ask me to sign away my country? It is your business to talk to us about spirit matters, and not to talk to us about parting with our land." Governor Stevens urged my father to sign his treaty, but he refused. "I will not sign your paper, he said; "you go where you please, so do I; you are not a child, I am no child; I can think for myself. No man can think for me. I have no other home than this. I will not give it up to any man. My people would have no home. Take away your paper. I will not touch it with my hand."

My father left the council. Some of the chiefs of the other bands of the Nez Percés signed the treaty, and then Governor Stevens gave them presents of blankets. My father cautioned his people to take no presents, for "after a while," he said, "they will claim that you have accepted pay for your country." Since that time four bands of the Nez Percés have received annuities from the United States. My father was invited to many councils, and they tried hard to make him sign the treaty, but he was firm as the rock, and would not sign away his home. His refusal caused a difference among the Nez Percés.

Eight years later (1863) was the next treaty council. A chief called Lawyer, because he was a great talker, took the lead in this council, and sold nearly all the Nez Percés country. My father was not there. He said to me: "when you go into council with the white man, always remember your country. Do not give it away. The white man will cheat you out of your home. I have taken no pay from the United States. I have never sold our land." In this treaty Lawyer acted without authority from our band. He had no right to sell the Wallowa (winding water) country. That had always belonged to my father's own people, and the other bands had never disputed our right to it. No other Indians ever claimed Wallowa.

In order to have all people understand how much land we owned, my father planted poles around it and said:

"Inside is the home of my people—the white man may take the land outside. Inside this boundary all our people were born. It circles around the graves of our fathers, and we will never give up these graves to any man."

The United States claimed they had bought all the Nez Percé's country outside of Lapwai Reservation, from Lawyer and other chiefs, but we continued to live on this land in peace until eight years ago, when white men began to come inside the bounds my father had set. We warned them against this great wrong, but they would not leave our land, and some bad blood was raised. The white men represented that we were going upon the warpath. They reported many things that were false.

The United States Government again asked for a treaty council. My father had become blind and feeble. He could no longer speak for his people. It was then that I took my father's place as chief. In this council I made my first speech to white men. I said to the agent who held the council:

"The white man has no right to come here and take our country."

"I did not want to come to this council, but I came hoping that we could save blood. The white man has no right to come here and take our country. We have never accepted any presents from the Government. Neither Lawyer nor any other chief had authority to sell this land. It has always belonged to my people. It came unclouded to them from our fathers, and we will defend this land as long as a drop of Indian blood warms the hearts of our men."

The agent said he had orders, from the Great White Chief at Washington, for us to go upon the Lapwai Reservation, and that if we obeyed he would help us in many ways. "You *must* move to the agency," he said. I answered him: "I will not. I do not need your help; we have plenty, and we are contented and happy if the white man will let us alone. The reservation is too small for so many people with all their stock. You can keep your presents; we can go to your towns and pay for all we need; we have plenty of horses and cattle to sell, and we won't have any help from you; we are free now; we can go where we please. Our fathers were born here. Here they lived, here they died, here are their graves. We will never leave them." The agent went away, and we had peace for a little while.

A Man Must Love His Father's Grave

Soon after this my father sent for me. I saw he was dying. I took his hand in mine. He said: "My son, my body is returning to my mother earth, and my spirit is going very soon to see the Great Spirit Chief. When I am gone, think of your country. You are the chief of these people. They look to you to guide them. Always remember that your father never sold his country. You must stop your ears whenever you are asked to sign a treaty selling your home. A few years more, and white men will be all around you. They have their eyes on this land. My son, never forget my dying words. This country holds your father's body. Never sell the bones of your father and your mother." I pressed my father's hand and told him I would protect his grave with my life. My father smiled and passed away to the spirit-land.

I buried him in that beautiful valley of winding waters. I love that land more than all the rest of the world. A man who would not love his father's grave is worse than a wild animal.

For a short time we lived quietly. But this could not last. White men had found gold in the mountains around the land of winding water. . . . We gave up some of our country to the white men, thinking that then we could have peace. We were mistaken. The white man would not let us alone. We could have avenged our wrongs many times, but we did not. . . .

On account of the treaty made by the other bands of the Nez Percés, the white men claimed my lands. We were troubled greatly by white men crowding over the line. Some of these were good men, and we lived on peaceful terms with them, but they were not all good.

We gave up some of our country to the white men, thinking that then we could have peace. We were mistaken.

Nearly every year the agent came over from Lapwai and ordered us on to the reservation. We always replied that we were satisfied to live in Wallowa. We were careful to refuse the presents or annuities which he offered.

Through all the years since the white men came to Wallowa we have been threatened and taunted by them and the treaty Nez Percés. They have given us no rest. We have had a few good friends among white men, and they have always advised my people to bear these taunts without fighting. Our young men were quick-tempered, and I have had great trouble in keeping them from doing rash things. I have carried a heavy load on my back ever since I was a boy. I learned then that we were but few, while the white men were many, and that we could not hold our own with them. We were like deer. They were like grizzly bears. We had a small country. Their country was large. We were contented to let things remain as the Great Spirit Chief made them. They were not; and would change the rivers and mountains if they did not suit them.

Year after year we have been threatened, but no war was made upon my people until General Howard came to our country two years ago and told us that he was the white war-chief of all that country. He said: "I have a great many soldiers at my back. I am going to bring them up here, and then I will talk to you again. I will not let white men laugh at me the next time I come. The country belongs to the Government, and I intend to make you go upon the reservation.". . .

I said to General Howard: ". . . I have been in a great many councils, but I am no wiser. We are all sprung from a woman, although we are unlike in many things. We can not be made over again. You are as you were made, and as you were made you can remain. We are just as we were made by the Great Spirit, and you can not change us; then why should children of one mother and one father quarrel—why should one try to cheat the other? I do not believe that the Great Spirit Chief gave one kind of men the right to tell another kind of men what they must do."

"The Great Spirit Chief made the world as it is . . . I do not see where [white men] get authority to say that we shall not live where he placed us."

General Howard replied: "You deny my authority, do you? You want to dictate to me, do you?"

Then one of my chiefs—Too-hool-hool-suit—rose in the council and said to General Howard: "The Great Spirit Chief made the world as it is, and as he wanted it, and he made a part of it for us to live upon. I do not see where you get authority to say that we shall not live where he placed us."

General Howard lost his temper and said: "Shut up! I don't want to hear any more of such talk. The law says you shall go upon the reservation to live, and I want you to do so, but you persist in disobeying the law" (meaning the treaty). "If you do not move, I will take the matter into my own hand, and make you suffer for your disobedience."

Too-hool-hool-suit answered: "Who are you, that you ask us to talk, and then tell me I sha'n't talk? Are you the Great

Spirit? Did you make the world? Did you make the sun? Did you make the rivers to run for us to drink? Did you make the grass to grow? Did you make all these things, that you talk to us as though we were boys? If you did, then you have the right to talk as you do.". . . You can arrest me, but you can not change me or make me take back what I have said.". . .

Too-hool-hool-suit was [a] prisoner for five days before he was released.

The council broke up for that day. On the next morning General Howard came to my lodge, and invited me to go with him and White-Bird and Looking-Glass, to look for land for my people. As we rode along we came to some good land that was already occupied by Indians and white people. General Howard, pointing to this land, said: "If you will come on to the reservation, I will give you these lands and move these people off."

I replied: "No. It would be wrong to disturb these people. I have no right to take their homes. I have never taken what did not belong to me. I will not now."

We rode all day upon the reservation, and found no good land unoccupied. . . .

In the council, next day, General Howard informed me, in a haughty spirit, that he would give my people *thirty days* to go back home, collect all their stock, and move on to the reservation, saying, "If you are not here in that time, I shall consider that you want to fight, and will send my soldiers to drive you on.". . .

I knew I had never sold my country, and that I had no land in Lapwai; but I did not want bloodshed. I did not want my people killed. I did not want anybody killed. . . .

I said in my heart that, rather than have war, I would give up my country. I would give up my father's grave. I would give up everything rather than have the blood of white men upon the hands of my people. . . .

I Cannot Understand So Many Chiefs

At last I was granted permission to come to Washington and bring my friend Yellow Bull and our interpreter with me. I am glad we came. I have shaken hands with a great many friends, but there are some things I want to know which no one seems able to explain. I cannot understand how the Government sends a man out to fight us . . . and then breaks his word. Such a Government has something wrong about it. I cannot understand why so many chiefs are allowed to talk so many different ways, and promise so many different things. I have seen the Great Father Chief (the President), the next Great Chief (Secretary of the Interior), the Commissioner Chief (Hayt), the Law Chief (General Butler), and many other law chiefs (Congressmen), and they all say they are my friends, and that I shall have justice, but while their mouths all talk right I do not understand why nothing is done for my people. I have heard talk and talk, but nothing is done. Good words do not last long unless they amount to something. Words do not pay for my dead people. They do not pay for my country, now overrun by white men. They do not protect my father's grave. They do not pay for all my horses and cattle. Good words will not give me back my children. Good words will not make good the promise of your War Chief General Miles. Good words will not give my people good health and stop them from dying. Good words will not get my people a home where they can live in peace and take care of themselves. I am tired of talk that comes to nothing. It makes my heart sick when I remember all the good words and all the broken promises. There has been too much talking by men who had no right to talk. Too many misrepresentations have been made, too many misunderstandings have come up between the white men about the Indians. If the white man wants to live in peace with the Indian he can live in peace. There need be no trouble. Treat all men alike. Give them all the same law. Give them all an even chance to live and grow. All men were made by the same Great Spirit Chief. They are all brothers. The earth is the mother of all people, and all people should have equal rights upon it. You might as well expect the rivers to run backward as that any man who was born a free man should be contented when penned up and denied liberty to go where he pleases. If you tie a horse to a stake, do you expect he will grow fat? If you pen an Indian up on a small spot of earth, and compel him to stay there, he will not be contented, nor will he grow and prosper. I have asked some of the great white chiefs where they get their authority to say to the Indian that he shall stay in one place, while he sees white men going where they please. They can not tell me.

Treat Us Like All Other Men

I only ask of the Government to be treated as all other men are treated. If I can not go to my own home, let me have a home in some country where my people will not die so fast. I would like to go to Bitter Root Valley. There my people would be healthy; where they are now they are dying. Three have died since I left my camp to come to Washington.

It makes my heart sick when I remember all the good words and all the broken promises.

When I think of our condition my heart is heavy. I see men of my race treated as outlaws and driven from country to country, or shot down like animals.

I know that my race must change. We can not hold our own with the white men as we are. We only ask an even chance to live as other men live. We ask to be recognized as men. We ask that the same law shall work alike on all men. If the Indian breaks the law, punish him by the law. If the white man breaks the law, punish him also.

Let me be a free man—free to travel, free to stop, free to work, free to trade where I choose, free to choose my own teachers, free to follow the religion of my fathers, free to think and talk and act for myself—and I will obey every law, or submit to the penalty.

Whenever the white man treats the Indian as they treat each other, then we will have no more wars. We shall all be alike—brothers of one father and one mother, with one sky above us and one country around us, and one government for all. Then the Great Spirit Chief who rules above will smile upon this land, and send rain to wash out the bloody spots made by brothers' hands from the face of the earth. For this time the Indian race are waiting and praying. I hope that no more groans of wounded men and women will ever go to the ear of the Great Spirit Chief above, and that all people may be one people.

In-mut-too-yah-lat-lat has spoken for his people.

3
Indians Should Be Christianized

Abraham Steiner

Abraham Steiner was a member of the *Unitas Fratrum,* or Unity of the Brethren, the oldest international Protestant denomination. Founded in Bohemia and Moravia in 1457, it "quickly spread across Europe, established missions in every continent, and now, under the name of the Moravian Church, finds its chief home in the United States. . . . It is missionary work that constitutes their most glorious achievement; and, among their many noble undertakings in this field, none surpassed the mission to the Delaware and Mohican Indians of the United States and Canada," according to Paul Wallace, editor of Steiner's journal.

In 1740 the first group of Pennsylvania Moravians founded Nazareth, Pennsylvania; the following year, on Christmas Eve, 1741, Bethlehem, Pennsylvania, was established. Once established, the Moravian colony set about establishing missions and schools among the Indians. Schooling was to be stressed along with religion.

In the spring of 1789 Abraham Steiner accompanied Johann Heckewelder, an elder of the Moravian church, while he made one of his many trips west from Bethlehem. The following viewpoint is taken from Steiner's journal account of these travels. The two men went to see about surveying the lands Congress had set aside for the Moravian convert of Indians on the Muskingum River in Ohio. In the journal we see what life was like on the unsettled Indian frontier in the years following the American Revolution. Also apparent is the arduous life of the missionary and the real joy of making converts.

From Abraham Steiner's account of travels with Johann Heckewelder, in *A Narrative of the Mission of the United Brethren Among the Delaware and Mohegan Indians . . .* , by Johann Heckewelder (New York: McCarty & Davis, 1820).

Abraham Steiner's Account of his Journey with Johann Heck-ewelder from Bethlehem to Pettquotting on the Huron River near Lake Erie, and Return. 1789.

[April] 21st. Half a mile beyond the ferry we came to Yellow Breeches Creek which, though sometimes a wild and dangerous stream, we were able to ride across without difficulty. 5 miles from Carlisle we saw a Presbyterian pulpit in the woods. These pulpits are built on a tree in the woods where people camp. A flight of three or four steps lead up to the pulpit, over which a small roof is built. At 1 o'clock in the afternoon we came to Carlisle, 16 miles from the ferry. We had a fine view of the place as we approached. This beautiful little town lies on an open plain. East of the town there are 5 long two-story buildings, each about 100 feet in length, built of brick, besides several smaller buildings, and an arsenal built of rough stone. During the war these buildings were put up by the States for workingmen attached to the army; they are, however, no longer maintained, and are now occupied only by Dr. Nesbitt, President of the local college, and a few young theological students. The town has about 350 handsome and for the most part two-story houses, most of which are built of handsome blue limestone, with which this vicinity abounds. The Courthouse is not large, but handsome, the prison small, and the market good. There are 3 churches, and the inhabitants, half of whom are German and half English, are mostly Presbyterians, Roman Catholics, German Lutherans and Reformed. The Methodists, too, have a meeting place here. There is a college here [Dickinson] but not in very good condition, and also two English schools; business is good, and there are many stores. There is a good printing press, and almost all trades are carried on here, in particular the making of nails and good beer. . . .

On the 22nd we rode 14 miles through dry land where there are no springs, to Shippensburg, where we had breakfast. . . . We saw several acquaintances here. We saw also our first packhorses. They put packs on them which they have to carry over the mountains. The drivers do not set off before 8 or 9 o'clock in the morning, but they drive all day till late in the evening. There are often 40 or 50 horses together. From here it is 10 miles to the foot of the Blue Mountain, where a German innkeeper lives named Kiefer. From this point on we had mountains to climb. There are 3 high ones here, one right after the other, which they call the Blue Mountains. A few years ago there was only a path over them, but now there is as good a road as can be expected on such mountains. . . .

The 23rd. We passed the place where Fort Littleton formerly stood. . . . Formerly Sideling Hill was much dreaded by travellers because of the rough steep road and the huge rocks on it. But here you can see what an efficient government can do in such a case. . . . There used to be very good hunting in these mountains and there are still many deer. . . . We ferried over the Juniata because the river was too high for fording. The road then follows a ridge; one has the Juniata on both sides. . . . On the north side of the road the bank is very high and steep, & the road runs close to the edge. Once, it is said, a man went over here with a wagon & 4 horses, & nothing has been heard of him since. . . . At night we came to Snakespring, 11 miles from the Crossing, and stopped at Diefenbach's, a German Innkeeper's. While we were on the road it rained fairly hard, but once we were inside the house there came a downpour with thunder & lightning. Snakespring is said to have received its name from the Indian traders, who used to have a trading post here. Once a lot of them got together here and had a celebration, during which they killed a snake, fried it in the fire & ate it, & afterwards called the place Snakespring.

On the 24th . . . we reached our friend Bonnet's, 4 miles beyond Bedford, where we stayed till next morning & were well looked after. . . . Here & on the adjoining plantation there are more than 200 acres of cleared pasture-land, and more can be cleared. Mr. Bonnet makes several 100 pounds a year from passing travelers for hay and pasturage, and some of his neighbors do almost as well. Here the great road to Pittsburg divides into two main roads, the one called the Pennsylvania Road [by way of Ligonier], the other the Glades Road [by way of Berlin]. . . .

On the 25th we had a good road for 5 miles farther till we came to Anderson's at the foot of the famous Allegheny Mountain. . . . A strong wind was blowing as we climbed, and it was still blowing hard while we were on top. The road up the mountain is rather stony, & all along the lower half small springs come out of the mountain on the left and run down the road. It is not particularly steep, and you can get up if you climb slowly and don't mind tired legs. Left of the road, all down the side of the mountain, the soil is very rich & this is called the "Garden Spot." It produces tall weeds, & all kinds of timber and shrubs are found here growing together. There are cherry, walnut, locust, sassafras, mulberry, ash, chestnut, hickory, elm, maple, beech, oak, aspen, etc. On the right hand side a beautiful little brook goes tumbling down. On the far side of the brook the mountain rises rather higher and the soil is poorer. Here are Spruce, white & pitch pine, cedar & boxwood. It is flat on top of the mountain, and it continues like that with some little variations to Laurel Hill, so that it may be said that Laurel Hill stands on Allegheny Mountain. The soil on the mountain top is mostly a black, rich loam, but it is cold; the grain often freezes, but grass grows in abundance. It is fairly well settled, and although there are not many plantations to be seen along the way, the people are already complaining that their neighbors are too close to them. . . .

On the 26th we could not get warm all day. We crossed Laurel Hill today. . . . It began to snow, & it kept on snowing until evening when the snow was 2 inches deep. Thunder & lightning accompanied the snow & it was intensely cold. . . . We spent the night with a German named Ried, who keeps a good inn. . . . Mr. Hufnagel & 2 other gentlemen from Greensburg also spent the night here. The former said a great many nice things about our Indian mission, condemned in the strongest terms the murder of the Indians on the Muskingum, & was angry because the ringleaders had not been punished.

A man named Steinmez told us that his neighbors . . . praise the Moravian Indians & say there are no better Christians than they.

On the 27th we went on to Greensburg. . . . Many Germans live in this neighborhood. . . . A man named Steinmez told us that his neighbors, who have driven cattle to Detroit, praise the Moravian Indians & say there are no better Christians than they. In this vicinity, which is called the German Settlement, the Indians committed many murders during the last war. We went on another 8 miles through beautiful country to a German by the name of Waldhauer, who would not let us go on. So we spent the night with him & rested well. . . . A lot of people from this area are moving to the Missury. They are having particular trouble with rascals who owe them money, slip quietly off to the Youghiogany, where boats are always ready to pull out, and go down from there by way of the Mononghahela & Ohio to the Mississippi. . . .

On the 28th we . . . reached Pittsburg by 3 o'clock. . . . General Gibson told us that his boat would leave in the morning for Kentucky & would stop at Marietta. We wanted to go along. But then one person advised us for it and another against it, until Br. Heckeweider found Mr. Isaac Williams, who lives in Sandusky and only recently has come from there. He said he had been sent with a "speech" from all the nations to Gov. St. Clair, which, however, as the Governor was not at home, he would take back again. This was the gist of the message: that the Indians will not allow the land which had been ceded at the last Treaty to be surveyed, and no forts are to be built on it, and, more particularly, they have made up their minds to kill all surveyors who go out. He added that the Indians say they were forced to the last Treaty. They neglected their fall hunting because of it; it lasted until winter, & they became poor, naked, & hungry. This drove them to accept certain terms in hopes of getting some food and clothing, but as they found themselves for the most part cheated, they merely laughed at the Treaty when they returned from it, and did not honor it at all. The Indians have decided to make an attack on the New England settlement on the Muskingum. They were resolved to fight for their land, and then if they lost it they would lose it like men. At this time there were many Indians on the Muskingum who were there only to keep watch. If we now surveyed the tract for the Moravian Indians on the Muskingum, it might cause trouble, & if soldiers were present it would be all the worse, & what would 20 or 30 soldiers be for the Indians lying in wait for them in the woods. Mr. Connelly from Detroit was present & confirmed this. They entreated us under no circumstances to survey the land, it would certainly cause trouble. They advised us, instead, to go to our Brethren at Pettquotting, where we could best inform ourselves about the matter. Not knowing what to do, we decided to stay here for a few days. All honest people here are sorry for the poor Indians, who lose their land without getting anything for it. They say the Treaty cost a lot, and most of the Indians got nothing. Some who were to have got something thought it was not even worth while to put out their hands for it, it was so small. . . .

On the 30th we were invited to breakfast with Mr. Nicholson, an "Interpreter of Indian languages," who advised us to survey our land, & would not hear of any danger. . . .

May 1st. Mr. Wilson, who had come from Washington [Pennsylvania] yesterday, brought us the certain news that the Indians on Dunker Creek had killed several white people and stolen some horses. He advised against surveying the land at this time, and so did almost everyone. So we prepared to go to Pettquotting. . . .

All honest people here are sorry for the poor Indians, who lose their land without getting anything for it.

On the 10th it rained. We met a number of Indians who were going with skins to Beaver Creek, where General Gibson had directed them to come for trading because many of them were afraid to go to Pittsburg. After them came Anton (Wellochalent), formerly one of the Brethren, but he had reverted. He had just now shot a bear. He gave us a ham from it. We let our party go on ahead. Br. Heckewelder reminded him of the grace he had once experienced. He replied that he had never intended to leave the Moravians, but, when his whole family was murdered, that not only grieved him but also so infuriated him that he resolved to go to war, & he had been weak enough to do so. Now he had avenged himself & had no longer any hatred of the white people. He often thought of going back to the Moravians, but believed he was too wicked. Br. Heckewelder said: "The thought of returning to the congregation comes from the Saviour, he has taken hold of you & will not easily let you go. He will forgive you everything if you turn to him." Anton said: "You speak words of comfort to me. I will soon return." And so we parted. Anton was once a very good man. He did much for the white people, saved their lives, & during the war brought them himself to safety, often at risk of his life. He had a good wife & lovely, promising children. These were all killed in the great massacre on the Muskingum. . . .

The 12th. In the morning 2 young Delaware Indians came to our camp. The father of one of them was a brother-in-law of the woman who was travelling with us. They were friendly & confirmed the report of the horse-stealing at Wheeling. The Delawares are said to have delivered a Speech to these Mingoes, to get them to mend their ways, but to no effect, & the Delawares are said to have gone quietly off because they saw it was no use. These same Mingoes are said to have stolen 11 horses from Mr. Ludlow, a surveyor, & then returned. On the way we saw the grave of an Indian who, at sugar-making in the spring, ate so much sugar that his stomach swelled and he died. . . .

On the 20th we came to the road that turns off to Pettquotting. . . . We met 2 Indians, who gave us directions about our road. The plains were becoming wetter and more extensive, broken only by an occasional long narrow strip of oak trees, the hollow ones being full of bees. Now and again we saw single large sandstones, and small round, stony hills, where innumerable crawfish live & make holes in the ground. Everywhere little round hillocks had been thrown up. Otherwise the whole region was as flat as a board. The horses walked on hard ground for miles, up to their knees in water, & under the water white violets grew. . . . 5 miles from Pettquotting we came into woods again and broken country. Better than a mile from the town was a peeled tree, on which, was written with charcoal in Delaware the whole verse, "The Saviour's blood & righteousness." This made us a good road sign. At last we saw the town before us. On a hill, at the fence of the nearest plantation, we called to the Indians working in the field. As soon as they recognized us, they dropped their hoes & ran to meet us. Several who were on the other side of the stream hurried across, & everybody welcomed us, accompanied us across the field to the river, & then over into the town, which we reached about 3 o'clock. Here we were welcomed by the Zeisbergers & the Edwards & Jung, & the Indian Brethren & Sisters swarmed about us until evening. It was an amazing sight to see a crowd of people who had once been heathen & are now true Christians & lovers of Jesus & his flock. The place is named Pettquotting after a high round hill, 5 miles from here. The town [New Salem, two miles from Milan] is set on a hill which is washed by the Huron River on the west, & has a deep, narrow valley on the east. The hill is fairly dry, but so narrow that not more than two rows of houses can stand on it, and these have only very small gardens or none at all. Towards the south the hill becomes a large, wet plain. Every cellar on this high, wet place has to have a drain. The schoolhouse is beautiful, with fireplaces on both sides, & a nice fence across the front. Not far from it, on the other side of the street, is the church. It is roomy, bark-covered, without board flooring & without windows, with 2 doors, good benches including some for the children, & candlesticks & candles. The bell hangs outside on a forked tree with a tiny roof built over it. The buildings in town are rather irregular & small, but most of them are well-built & all give protection against rain & cold. There are, however, no glass windows here, only a few paper ones. Those who have any glass save it. The graveyard is near the town, to the southeast. When a grave is dug in the wet season, it stands full of water. But there is no better place. It is 3 1/2 miles by land to Lake Erie northeast of here, and 5 1/2 miles by water down the river. Huron River is here about 12 rods wide, 30 feet deep. It is also called Bald Eagle Creek from a large eagle's nest found at the rivermouth. This is the only drinking water. In summer, when it is quiet, the water is stagnant & bad. When the winds blow in from the lake, the lake water comes up the river to above the town, & this is the best drinking water. The bottoms down river are for the most part wet; up river they are dry & rich, with not many swamps. They produce everything in abundance when not too wet. All the high land is too wet. Trees of all the usual kinds grow here. Sugar trees, ginseng, & deer are scarce in this vicinity. They trap many raccoons and also beaver & otter here. There are bears, too, and many bees in the woods. There are plenty of fish in the river, especially very large catfish, and at times there are many geese & ducks. The Indians have horses, cattle, chickens, & many pigs. They can live well if they plant enough.

It was an amazing sight to see a crowd of people who had once been heathen & are now true Christians & lovers of Jesus & his flock.

On Ascension Day, the 21st, we had only 2 services as it was rainy. We consulted the Brethren about our problem. They we against our surveying the land on the Muskingum at this time but they wanted the opinion and advice of some of the Assistants. During the spring there had been a great uproar among some of the bad Indians at the thought of the Christians now moving to the Muskingum. They had settled down, but if the land were now surveyed they would be in an uproar again and might ruin the whole congregation. If someone were connected with the business whom they knew to be a former teacher, it would be so much the worse. We should not tell the Indians why we were here, for fear it might get to the ears of the bad Indians. West of here live wicked bands among whom are utterly godless whites & Indians. They are always in a stir, and are said to live in a pitiful condition. Br. David was very busy this week preparing his address for Holy Communion. . . .

West of here live wicked bands among whom are utterly godless whites & Indians.

The 23rd. We had Communion in the evening. All communicants came afterwards to Br. David's room. The Brethren all kissed one another, the Sisters did the same among themselves, & Brethren & Sisters shook hands with one another in mutual fellowship. It is a great thing to see a congregation drawn from raw heathendom fully enjoying the reward & bounties of Jesus, & loving one another like true Christians.

On the 25th a conference was held with Samuel & Wilhelm. Much as they wished to see our affair succeed & to help us themselves, they were nevertheless of opinion we should drop the matter for the time being. Their reasons were exactly the same as those the white Brethren had advanced. They thought that, since the Indians did not want the Christians to go to the Muskingum and supposed they would have to as soon as the land was surveyed, all who had relatives at this place would take them away and very likely some wicked band would come and take the rest away. They said: "You cannot conceive how closely they watch us, and they are worse than you imagine. They are determined that no surveyor shall set foot on that land. Perhaps the matter will be cleared up after the Council meets at Deep River near Detroit, where Brant is expected." We discussed the matter further during the week, and came to the conclusion:

"God forbid! It were better the land were never surveyed than that the least harm should befall the mission. The land should rather be sacrificed for the mission than the mission for the land.". . .

The land should rather be sacrificed for the mission than the mission for the land.

The 31st was Pentecost, which the Indians observe as an important day. There was a baptism of 3 Brethren and 1 Sister. Two of those baptized were sons of William Henry, who formerly was known as Killbuck or Gelelemind. One of them had lived 4 years at Princeton, & had attended the college there. The persons baptized were dressed in white & wore blue gowns over their garments because it was cool. Reed mats were spread before them. After an address by Br. David, the sacristans hauled water in 4 buckets with a tin basin in each. The men & women Assistants removed their gowns, & after they had worshiped they were led into Br. David's house & had dry clothes put on them. When it was all over, all the Brethren kissed the newly baptized Brethren, & the Sisters kissed the newly baptized Sister. The Brethren shook hands with the Sister, & the Sisters shook hands with the Brethren. Everyone was happy to see new partakers in the blessedness they themselves enjoyed. Things go very well, on the whole, among the young people here. A great longing fires them to surrender themselves to Him who gave His life for them. An Indian is an independent person who is not inclined to seek advice nor to change his mind to please anyone. It is a tremendous thing when such a one decides to surrender himself to Jesus, and still more so when it is a young Indian who is just as independent & who in addition has to fight the temptations of the world. Towards evening there was a lovefeast for the whole congregation. The church was crowded. There were some Chippewas present, who had come because they had heard that today was Sunday. At the lovefeast everything went off very well. Br. David told the Indians about the congregations at Bethlehem & other places, & assured them they were remembered by them. It was a happy day for the Indian congregation. I should mention with what eagerness the Indians go to school to learn reading, writing, & hymns. Br. David conducts school here by himself, in various classes, from morning till night. School stops only during the busiest planting & harvesting seasons. Men, women, & children attend it. At other times you see, here & there, a little group in a corner, learning reading and hymns from one another. You may hear them in the evening singing hymns in their houses until late at night.

On the 1st of June, from morning till noon, there were Indians with us saying good-bye. When we left at 2 o'clock, they assembled once more and went through it all over again. The whole hill, from the houses on down, was covered with people following us with their eyes as long as they could. . . .

On the 9th we forded Muddy Run, crossed some plains, & then came to the best high land we had seen on our whole journey. At 5 o'clock we reached the Allegheny, & before dark were again in Pittsburg,—

It is a tremendous thing when such a one decides to surrender himself to Jesus, and still more so when it is a young Indian.

Where we stayed the 10th & 11th. We could do little business here. The people in whom we were chiefly interested were busy listening to the inquiry then being conducted in the church by 6 pastors from the neighbourhood into the dispute between the Presbyterian congregation and their pastor. Messrs. Morrison & Connelly told us they thanked God they had returned safely. They had gone in the spring to the mouth of the Cayahaga with flour, & thought themselves fortunate not to have known at the time the danger they were in. Had the war parties that were lying in wait not missed them, they would have been at their mercy. Everybody, by the way, advised us to take the advice of our Brethren & not survey the land at this time. We said good-bye to the Indian Brethren & our hosts, &—

On the 12th left Pittsburg. . . .

On the 24th, [June] arrived in Bethlehem.

4

Indians Wish to Keep Their Own Religion

Charles Alexander Eastman

When the Santee Sioux of Minnesota rose up against white settlers in 1862, government retaliation was swift. Many of the Sioux fled into exile in Canada; among them was four-year-old Charles Alexander Eastman, born "Pitiful Last" but later called "Ohiyesa—The Winner." He did not see a white person until he was sixteen. Later, he attended Dartmouth College and, in 1890, earned his medical degree from Boston University. He thus lived in and observed both worlds—the Indians' and the whites'. This is evident in the following viewpoint explaining native American religious beliefs, excerpted from Eastman's book *The Soul of the Indian,* published in 1911.

The original attitude of the American Indian toward the Eternal, the "Great Mystery" that surrounds and embraces us, was as simple as it was exalted. To him it was the supreme conception, bringing with it the fullest measure of joy and satisfaction possible in this life.

The worship of the "Great Mystery" was silent, solitary, free from all self-seeking. It was silent, because all speech is of necessity feeble and imperfect; therefore the souls of my ancestors ascended to God in wordless adoration. It was solitary, because they believed that He is nearer to us in solitude, and there were no priests authorized to come between a man and his Maker. None might exhort or confess or in any way meddle with the religious experience of another. Among us all men were created sons of God and stood

From *The Soul of the Indian,* by Charles Alexander Eastman (Boston: Houghton Mifflin, 1911).

erect, as conscious of their divinity. Our faith might not be formulated in creeds, nor forced upon any who were unwilling to receive it; hence there was no preaching, proselyting, nor persecution, neither were there any scoffers or atheists.

Our [Indian] faith might not be formulated in creeds, nor forced upon any who were unwilling to receive it.

There were no temples or shrines among us save those of nature. Being a natural man, the Indian was intensely poetical. He would deem it sacrilege to build a house for Him who may be met face to face in the mysterious, shadowy aisles of the primeval forest, or on the sunlit bosom of virgin prairies, upon dizzy spires and pinnacles of naked rock, and yonder in the jeweled vault of the night sky! He who enrobes Himself in filmy veils of cloud, there on the rim of the visible world where our Great-Grandfather Sun kindles his evening camp-fire, He who rides upon the rigorous wind of the north, or breathes forth His spirit upon aromatic southern airs, whose war-canoe is launched upon majestic rivers and inland seas—He needs no lesser cathedral!

Hambeday

That solitary communion with the Unseen which was the highest expression of our religious life is partly described in the word *hambeday*, literally "mysterious feeling," which has been variously translated "fasting" and "dreaming." It may better be interpreted as "consciousness of the divine."

The first *hambeday*, or religious retreat, marked an epoch in the life of the youth, which may be compared to that of confirmation or conversion in Christian experience. Having first prepared himself by means of the purifying vapor-bath, and cast off as far as possible all human or fleshly influences, the young man sought out the noblest height, the most commanding summit in all the surrounding region. Knowing that God sets no Value upon material things, he took with him no offerings or sacrifices other than symbolic objects, such as paints and tobacco. Wishing to appear before Him in all humility, he wore no clothing save his moccasins and breech-clout. At the solemn hour of sunrise or sunset he took up his position, overlooking the glories of earth and facing the "Great Mystery" and there he remained, naked, erect, silent, and motionless, exposed to the elements and forces of His arming, for a night and a day to two days and nights, but rarely longer. Sometimes he would chant a hymn without words, or offer the ceremonial "filled pipe." In this holy trance or ecstasy the Indian mystic found his highest happiness and the motive power of his existence.

When he returned to the camp, he must remain at a distance until he had again entered the vapor-bath and prepared himself for intercourse with his fellows. Of the vision or sign vouchsafed to him he did not speak, unless it had included some commission which must be publicly fulfilled. Sometimes an old man, standing upon the brink of eternity, might reveal to a chosen few the oracle of his long-past youth.

What Is the Nature of Virtue?

The native American has been generally despised by his white conquerors for his poverty and simplicity. They forget, perhaps, that his religion forbade the accumulation of wealth and the enjoyment of luxury. To him, as to other single-minded men in every age and race, from Diogenes to the brothers of Saint Francis, from the Montanists to the Shakers, the love of possessions has appeared a snare, and the burdens of a complex society a source of needless peril and temptation. Furthermore, it was the rule of his life to share the fruits of his skill and success with his less fortunate brothers. Thus he kept his spirit free from the clog of pride, cupidity, or envy, and carried out, as he believed, the divine decree—a matter profoundly important to him.

[The Indian's] religion forbade the accumulation of wealth and the enjoyment of luxury.

It was not, then, wholly from ignorance or improvidence that he failed to establish permanent towns and to develop a material civilization. To the untutored sage, the concentration of population was the prolific mother of all evils, moral no less than physical. He argued that food is good, while surfeit kills; that love is good, but lust destroys; and not less dreaded than the pestilence following upon crowded and unsanitary dwellings was the loss of spiritual power inseparable from too close contact with one's fellow-men. All who have lived much out of doors know that there is a magnetic and nervous force that accumulates in solitude and that is quickly dissipated by life in a crowd; and even his enemies have recognized the fact that for a certain innate power and self-poise, wholly independent of circumstances, the American Indian is unsurpassed among men.

The red man divided mind into two parts,—the spiritual mind and the physical mind. The first is pure spirit, concerned only with the essence of things, and it was this he sought to strengthen by spiritual prayer, during which the body is subdued by fasting and hardship. In this type of prayer there was no beseeching of favor or help. All matters of personal or selfish concern, as success in hunting or warfare, relief from sickness, or the sparing of a beloved life, were definitely relegated to the plane of the lower or material mind, and all ceremonies, charms, or incantations designed to secure a benefit or to avert a danger, were recognized as emanating from the physical self.

Religious Symbolism

The rites of this physical worship, again, were wholly symbolic, and the Indian no more worshiped the Sun than the Christian adores the Cross. The Sun and the Earth, by an obvious parable, holding scarcely more of poetic metaphor than of scientific truth, were in his view the parents of all organic life. From the Sun, as the universal father, proceeds the quickening principle in nature, and in the patient and fruitful womb of our mother, the Earth, are hidden embryos of plants and men. Therefore our reverence and love for them was really an imaginative extension of our love for our immediate parents, and with this sentiment of filial piety was joined a willingness to appeal to them, as to a father, for such good gifts as we may desire. This is the material or physical prayer.

The elements and majestic forces in nature, Lightning, Wind, Water, Fire, and Frost, were regarded with awe as spiritual powers, but always secondary and intermediate in character. We believed that the spirit pervades all creation and that every creature possesses a soul in some degree, though not necessarily a soul conscious of itself. The tree, the waterfall, the grizzly bear, each is an embodied Force, and as such an object of reverence.

The Indian loved to come into sympathy and spiritual communion with his brothers of the animal kingdom, whose inarticulate souls had for him something of the sinless purity that we attribute to the innocent and irresponsible child. He had faith in their instincts, as in a mysterious wisdom given from above; and while he humbly accepted the supposedly voluntary sacrifice of their bodies to preserve his own, he paid homage to their spirits in prescribed prayers and offerings.

The Importance of the Supernatural

In every religion there is an element of the supernatural, varying with the influence of pure reason over its devotees. The Indian was a logical and clear thinker upon matters within the scope of his understanding, but he had not yet charted the vast field of nature or expressed her wonders in terms of science. With his limited knowledge of cause and effect, he saw miracles on every hand,—the miracle of life in seed and egg, the miracle of death in lightning flash and in the swelling deep! Nothing of the marvelous could astonish him; as that a beast should speak, or the sun stand still. The virgin birth would appear scarcely more miraculous than is the birth of every child that comes into the world, or the miracle of the loaves and fishes excite more wonder than the harvest that springs from a single ear of corn.

Our American Indian myths and hero stories are perhaps, in themselves, quite as credible as those of the Hebrews of old.

Who may condemn his superstition? Surely not the devout Catholic, or even Protestant missionary, who teaches Bible miracles as literal fact! The logical man must either deny all miracles or none, and our American Indian myths and hero stories are perhaps, in themselves, quite as credible as those of the Hebrews of old. If we are of the modern type of mind, that sees in natural law a majesty and grandeur far more impressive than any solitary infraction of it could possibly be, let us not forget that, after all, science has not explained everything. We have still to face the ultimate miracle,—the origin and principle of life! Here is the supreme mystery that is the essence of worship, without which there can be no religion, and in the presence of this mystery our attitude cannot be very unlike that of the natural philosopher, who beholds with awe the Divine in all creation.

It is simple truth that the Indian did not, so long as his native philosophy held sway over his mind, either envy or desire to imitate the splendid achievements of the white man. In his own thought he rose superior to them! He scorned them, even as a lofty spirit absorbed in its stem task rejects the soft beds, the luxurious food, the pleasure-worshiping dalliance of a rich neighbor. It was clear to him that virtue and happiness are independent of these things, if not incompatible with them.

An Evaluation of Christianity

There was undoubtedly much in primitive Christianity to appeal to this man, and Jesus' hard sayings to the rich and about the rich would have been entirely comprehensible to him. Yet the religion that is preached in our churches and practiced by our congregations, with its element of display and self-aggrandizement, its active proselytism, and its open contempt of all religions but its own, was for a long time extremely repellent. To his simple mind, the professionalism of the pulpit, the paid exhorter, the moneyed church, was an unspiritual and unedifying thing, and it was not until his spirit was broken and his moral and physical constitution undermined by trade, conquest, and strong drink, that Christian missionaries obtained any real hold upon him. Strange as it may seem, it is true that the proud pagan in his secret soul despised the good men who came to convert and to enlighten him!

It is true that the proud pagan in his secret soul despised the good men who came to convert and to enlighten him!

Nor were its publicity and its Phariseeism the only elements in the alien religion that offended the red man. To him, it appeared shocking and almost incredible that there were among this people who claimed superiority many irreligious, who did not even pretend to profess the national faith. Not only did they not profess it, but they stooped so low as to insult their God with profane and sacrilegious speech! In our own tongue His name was not spoken aloud, even with utmost reverence, much less lightly or irreverently.

More than this, even in those white men who professed religion we found much inconsistency of conduct. They spoke much of spiritual things, while seeking only the material. They bought and sold everything: time, labor, personal independence, the love of woman, and even the ministrations of their holy faith! The lust for money, power, and conquest so characteristic of the Anglo-Saxon race did not escape moral condemnation at the hands of his untutored judge, nor did he fail to contrast this conspicuous trait of the dominant race with the spirit of the meek and lowly Jesus.

He might in time come to recognize that the drunkards and licentious among white men, with whom he too frequently came in contact, were condemned by the white man's religion as well, and must not be held to discredit it. But it was not so easy to overlook or to excuse national bad faith. When distinguished emissaries from the Father at Washington, some of them ministers of the gospel and even bishops, came to the Indian nations, and pledged to them in solemn treaty the national honor, with prayer and mention of their God; and when such treaties, so made, were promptly and shamelessly broken, is it strange that the action should arouse not only anger, but contempt? The historians of the white race admit that the Indian was never the first to repudiate his oath. . . .

The Unwritten Scriptures

A missionary once undertook to instruct a group of Indians in the truths of his holy religion. He told them of the creation of the earth in six days, and of the fall of our first parents by eating an apple.

The courteous savages listened attentively, and, after thanking him, one related in his turn a very ancient tradition concerning the origin of the maize. But the missionary plainly showed his disgust and disbelief, indignantly saying: "What I delivered to you were sacred truths, but this that you tell me is mere fable and falsehood!"

"My brother," gravely replied the offended Indian, "it

seems that you have not been well grounded in the rules of civility. You saw that we, who practice these rules, believed your stories; why, then, do you refuse to credit ours?"

Every religion has its Holy Book, and ours was a mingling of history, poetry, and prophecy, of precept and folklore, even such as the modern reader finds within the covers of his Bible. This Bible of ours was our whole literature, a living Book, sowed as precious seed by our wisest sages, and springing anew in the wondering eyes and upon the innocent lips of little children. Upon its hoary wisdom of proverb and fable, its mystic and legendary lore thus sacredly preserved and transmitted from father to son, was based in large part our customs and philosophy.

Naturally magnanimous and open-minded, the red man prefers to believe that the Spirit of God is not breathed into man alone, but that the whole created universe is a sharer in the immortal perfection of its Maker. His imaginative and poetic mind, like that of the Greek, assigns to every mountain, tree, and spring its spirit, nymph, or divinity, either beneficent or mischievous. The heroes and demigods of Indian tradition reflect the characteristic trend of his thought, and his attribution of personality and will to the elements, the sun and stars, and all animate or inanimate nature.

5

Indians Should Join Together in War Against the Whites

Tecumseh

In the early 1800s, the famous Shawnee Indian chief Tecumseh met with nearly every tribe east of the Rocky Mountains to argue that they should join together to fight the whites who were taking their land. In the following speech, Tecumseh addresses members of the Choctaw and Chickasaw tribes and attempts to convince them to join together with other tribes in order to make war against the Americans. In 1811, American forces under William Henry Harrison destroyed Tecumseh's community of Prophetstown in what has become known as the Battle of Tippecanoe. During the War of 1812, Tecumseh joined the British to fight against the Americans and was killed in 1813.

In view of questions of vast importance, have we met together in solemn council tonight. Nor should we here debate whether we have been wronged and injured, but by what measures we should avenge ourselves; for our merciless oppressors, having long since planned out their proceedings, are not about to make, but have and are still making attacks upon our race who have as yet come to no resolution. Nor are we ignorant by what steps, and by what gradual advances, the whites break in upon our neighbors. Imagining themselves to be still undiscovered, they show themselves the less audacious because you are insensible. The whites are already nearly a match for us all united, and too strong for any one tribe alone

From Tecumseh's speech to the Choctaw and Chickasaw tribes, as recorded in *History of Fort Wayne*, by Wallace A. Brice (Fort Wayne, IN: D.W. Jones, 1868).

to resist; so that unless we support one another with our collective and united forces; unless every tribe unanimously combines to give check to the ambition and avarice of the whites, they will soon conquer us apart and disunited, and we will be driven away from our native country and scattered as autumnal leaves before the wind.

We will be driven away from our native country and scattered as autumnal leaves before the wind.

But have we not courage enough remaining to defend our country and maintain our ancient independence? Will we calmly suffer the white intruders and tyrants to enslave us? Shall it be said of our race that we knew not how to extricate ourselves from the three most dreadful calamities—folly, inactivity and cowardice? But what need is there to speak of the past? It speaks for itself and asks, Where today is the Pequod? Where the Narragansetts, the Mohawks, Pocanokets, and many other once powerful tribes of our race? They have vanished before the avarice and oppression of the white men, as snow before a summer sun. In the vain hope of alone defending their ancient possessions, they have fallen in the wars with the white men. Look abroad over their once beautiful country, and what see you now? Naught but the ravages of the pale face destroyers meet our eyes.

Tecumseh

So it will be with you Choctaws and Chickasaws! Soon your mighty forest trees, under the shade of whose wide spreading branches you have played in infancy, sported in boyhood, and now rest your wearied limbs after the fatigue of the chase, will be cut down to fence in the land which the white intruders dare to call their own. Soon their broad roads will pass over the grave of your fathers, and the place of their rest will be blotted out forever. The annihilation of our race is at hand unless we unite in one common cause against the common foe. Think not, brave Choctaws and Chickasaws, that you can remain passive and indifferent to the common danger, and thus escape the common fate. Your people, too, will soon be as falling leaves and scattering clouds before their blighting breath. You, too, will be driven away from your native land and ancient domains as leaves are driven before the wintry storms.

War or Extermination

Sleep not longer, O Choctaws and Chickasaws, in false security and delusive hopes. Our broad domains are fast escaping from our grasp. Every year our white intruders become more greedy, exacting, oppressive and overbearing. Every year contentions spring up between them and our people and when blood is shed we have to make atonement whether right or wrong, at the cost of the lives of our greatest chiefs, and the yielding up of large tracts of our lands. Before the palefaces came among us, we enjoyed the happiness of unbounded freedom, and were acquainted with neither riches, wants nor oppression. How is it now? Wants and oppression are our lot; for are we not controlled in everything, and dare we move without asking, by your leave? Are we not being stripped day by day of the little that remains of our ancient liberty? Do they not even kick and strike us as they do their black-faces? How long will it be before they will tie us to a post and whip us, and make us work for them in their corn fields as they do them? Shall we wait for that moment or shall we die fighting before submitting to such ignominy?

The annihilation of our race is at hand unless we unite in one common cause against the common foe.

Have we not for years had before our eyes a sample of their designs, and are they not sufficient harbingers of their future determinations? Will we not soon be driven from our respective countries and the graves of our ancestors? Will not the bones of our dead be plowed up, and their graves be turned into fields? Shall we calmly wait until they become so numerous that we will no longer be able to resist oppression? Will we wait to be destroyed in our turn, without making an effort worthy of our race? Shall we give up our homes, our country, bequeathed to us by the Great Spirit, the graves of our dead, and everything that is dear and sacred to us, without a struggle? I know you will cry with me: Never! Never! Then let us by unity of action destroy them all, which we now can do, or drive them back whence they came. War or extermination is now our only choice. Which do you choose? I know your answer. Therefore, I now call on you, brave Choctaws and Chickasaws, to assist in the just cause of liberating our race from the grasp of our faithless invaders and heartless oppressors. The white usurpation in our common country must be stopped, or we, its rightful owners, be forever destroyed and wiped out as a race of people. I am now at the head of many warriors backed by the strong arm of English soldiers. Choctaws and Chickasaws, you have too long borne with grievous usurpation inflicted by the arrogant Americans. Be no longer their dupes. If there be one here tonight who believes that his rights will not sooner or later be taken from him by the avaricious American palefaces, his ignorance ought to excite pity, for he knows little of the character of our common foe.

Every year our white intruders become more greedy, exacting, oppressive and overbearing.

And if there be one among you mad enough to undervalue the growing power of the white race among us, let him tremble in considering the fearful woes he will bring down upon our entire race, if by his criminal indifference he assists the designs of our common enemy against our common country. Then listen to the voice of duty, of honor, of nature and of your endangered country. Let us form one body, one heart, and defend to the last warrior our country, our homes, our liberty, and the graves of our fathers.

Grounds of Complaint

Choctaws and Chickasaws, you are among the few of our

race who sit indolently at ease. You have indeed enjoyed the reputation of being brave, but will you be indebted for it more from report than fact? Will you let the whites encroach upon your domains even to your very door before you will assert your rights in resistance? Let no one in this council imagine that I speak more from malice against the paleface Americans than just grounds of complaint. Complaint is just toward friends who have failed in their duty; accusation is against enemies guilty of injustice. And surely, if any people ever had, we have good and just reasons to believe we have ample grounds to accuse the Americans of injustice; especially when such great acts of injustice have been committed by them upon our race, of which they seem to have no manner of regard, or even to reflect. They are a people fond of innovations, quick to contrive and quick to put their schemes into effectual execution no matter how great the wrong and injury to us; while we are content to preserve what we already have. Their designs are to enlarge their possessions by taking yours in turn; and will you, can you longer dally, O Choctaws and Chickasaws?

Do you imagine that that people will not continue longest in the enjoyment of peace who timely prepare to vindicate themselves, and manifest a determined resolution to do themselves right whenever they are wronged? Far otherwise. Then haste to the relief of our common cause, as by consanguinity of blood you are bound; lest the day be not far distant when you will be left singlehanded and alone to the cruel mercy of our most inveterate foe.

6

Indians Should Live in Peace with the Whites

Pushmataha

In response to Shawnee leader Tecumseh's call for the Choctaws and Chickasaws to join together to fight the Americans, Choctaw leader Pushmataha urged his people to vote for peace. In the following speech, which he gave in 1811, Pushmataha reminds them that the Choctaws have always enjoyed peaceful and profitable relations with their white neighbors and would be better served to ignore Tecumseh's pleas. Pushmataha went on to fight on the American side in the War of 1812 and maintained friendly relations with his white neighbors until his death in 1824. Although the Choctaws remained loyal to the Americans, they became the first of the "Five Civilized Tribes"—so-named because they adopted many aspects of European culture—to be affected by the 1830 Indian Removal Act, a federal law that authorized the removal all Indians from the Southeast.

A ttention, my good red warriors! Hear ye my brief remarks.

The great Shawnee orator [Tecumseh] has portrayed in vivid picture the wrongs inflicted on his and other tribes by the ravages of the paleface. The candor and fervor of his eloquent appeal breathe the conviction of truth and sincerity, and, as kindred tribes, naturally we sympathize with the misfortunes of his people. I do not come before you in any disputation either for or against these charges. It is not my purpose to contradict any of these allegations against the

From Pushmataha's speech to his people in 1811 as reprinted in *Indian Oratory: Famous Speeches by Noted Indian Chieftains*, edited by W.C. Vanderwerth (Norman: University of Oklahoma Press, 1971).

white man, but neither am I here to indulge in any indiscreet denunciation of him which might bring down upon my people unnecessary difficulty and embarrassment.

The distinguished Shawnee sums up his eloquent appeal to us with this direct question:

"Will you sit idly by, supinely awaiting complete and abject submission, or will you die fighting beside your brethren, the Shawnees, rather than submit to such ignominy?"

These are plain words and it is well they have been spoken, for they bring the issue squarely before us. Mistake not, this language means war. And war with whom, pray? War with some band of marauders who have committed their depredations against the Shawnees? War with some alien host seeking the destruction of the Choctaws and Chickasaws? Nay, my fellow tribesmen. None of these are the enemy we will be called on to meet. If we take up arms against the Americans we must of necessity meet in deadly combat our daily neighbors and associates in this part of the country near our homes.

The Choctaws and the Americans

If Tecumseh's words be true, and we doubt them not, then the Shawnee's experience with the whites has not been the same as that of the Choctaws. These white Americans buy our skins, our corn, our cotton, our surplus game, our baskets, and other wares, and they give us in fair exchange their cloth, their guns, their tools, implements, and other things which the Choctaws need but do not make. It is true we have befriended them, but who will deny that these acts of friendship have been abundantly reciprocated? They have given us cotton gins, which simplify the spinning and sale of our cotton; they have encouraged and helped us in the production of our crops; they have taken many of our wives into their homes to teach them useful things, and pay them for their work while learning; they teach our children to read and write from their books. You all remember the dreadful epidemic visited upon us last winter. During its darkest hours these neighbors whom we are now urged to attack responded generously to our needs. They doctored our sick; they clothed our suffering; they fed our hungry; and where is the Choctaw or Chickasaw delegation who has ever gone to St. Stephens with a worthy cause and been sent away empty handed? So, in marked contrast with the experiences of the Shawnees, it will be seen that the whites and Indians in this section are living on friendly and mutually beneficial terms.

The whites and Indians in this section are living on friendly and mutually beneficial terms.

Forget not, O Choctaws and Chickasaws, that we are bound in peace to the Great White Father at Washington by a sacred treaty and the Great Spirit will punish those who break their word. The Great White Father has never violated that treaty and the Choctaws have never been driven to the necessity of taking up the tomahawk against him or his children. Therefore the question before us tonight is not the avenging of any wrongs perpetrated against us by the whites, for the Choctaws and Chickasaws have no such cause, either real or imaginary, but rather it is a question of carrying on that record of fidelity and justice for which our forefathers ever proudly stood, and doing that which is best calculated to promote the welfare of our own people. Yea, my fellow tribesmen, we are a just people. We do not take up the warpath without a just cause and honest purpose. Have we that just cause against our white neighbors, who have taken nothing from us except by fair bargain and exchange? Is this a just recompense for their assistance to us in our agricultural and other pursuits? Is this to be their gracious reward for teaching our children from their books? Shall this be considered the Choctaws' compensation for feeding our hungry, clothing our needy, and administering to our sick? Have we, O Choctaws and Chickasaws, descended to the low estate of ruthlessly breaking the faith of a sacred treaty? Shall our forefathers look back from the happy hunting grounds only to see their unbroken record for justice, gratitude, and fidelity thus rudely repudiated and abruptly abandoned by an unworthy offspring?

War Is an Awful Thing

We Choctaws and Chickasaws are a peaceful people, making our subsistence by honest toil; but mistake not, my Shawnee brethren, we are not afraid of war. Neither are we strangers to war, as those who have undertaken to encroach upon our rights in the past may abundantly testify. We are thoroughly familiar with war in all its details and we know full well all its horrible consequences. It is unnecessary for me to remind you, O Choctaws and Chickasaws, veteran braves of many fierce conflicts in the past, that war is an awful thing. If we go into this war against the Americans, we must be prepared to accept its inevitable results. Not only will it foretoken deadly conflict with neighbors and death to warriors, but it will mean suffering for our women, hunger and starvation for our children, grief for our loved ones, and devastation of our beloved homes. Notwithstanding these difficulties, if the cause be just, we should not hesitate to defend our rights to the last man, but before that fatal step is irrevocably taken, it is well that we fully understand and seriously consider the full portent and consequences of the act.

The People's Decision

Hear me, O Choctaws and Chickasaws, for I speak truly for your welfare. It is not the province of your chiefs to settle these important questions. As a people, it is your prerogative to have either peace or war, and as one of your chiefs, it is mine simply to counsel and advise. Therefore, let me admonish you that this critical period is no time to cast aside your wits and let blind impulse sway; be not driven like dumb brutes by the frenzied harangue of this wonderful Shawnee orator; let your good judgment rule and ponder seriously before breaking bonds that have served you well and ere you change conditions which have brought peace and happiness to your wives, your sisters, and your children. I would not undertake to dictate the course of one single Choctaw warrior. Permit me to speak for the moment, not as your chief but as a Choctaw warrior, weighing this question beside you. As such I shall exercise my calm, deliberate judgment in behalf of those most dear to me and dependent on me, and I shall not suffer my reason to be swept away by this eloquent recital of alleged wrongs which I know naught of. I deplore this war, I earnestly hope it may be averted, but if it be forced upon us I shall take my stand with those who have stood by my people in the past and will be found fighting beside our good friends of St. Stephens and surrounding country. I have finished. I call on all Choctaws and Chickasaws indorsing my sentiments to cast their tomahawks on this side of the council fire with me.

[The majority of listeners did support Pushmataha. Tecumseh responded by calling Pushmataha a coward and Pushmataha made the following rebuttal.]

The Americans have been our friends and we shall stand by them.

Halt, Tecumseh! Listen to me. You have come here, as you have often gone elsewhere, with a purpose to involve peaceful people in unnecessary trouble with their neighbors. Our people have had no undue friction with the whites. Why? Because we have had no leaders stirring up strife to serve their selfish, personal ambitions. You heard me say that our people are a peaceful people. They make their way, not by ravages upon their neighbors but by honest toil. In that regard they have nothing in common with you. I know your history well. You are a disturber. You have ever been a trouble maker. When you have found yourself unable to pick a quarrel with the white man, you have stirred up strife between different tribes of your own race. Not only that, you are a monarch and unyielding tyrant within your own domain; every Shawnee man, woman, and child must bow in humble submission to your imperious will. The Choctaws and Chickasaws have no monarchs. Their chieftains do not undertake the mastery of their people, but rather are they the people's servants, elected to serve the will of the majority. The majority has spoken on this question and it has spoken against your contention. Their decision has therefore become the law of the Choctaws and Chickasaws and Pushmataha will see that the will of the majority so recently expressed is rigidly carried out to the letter.

If, after this decision, any Choctaw should be so foolish as to follow your imprudent advice and enlist to fight against the Americans, thereby abandoning his own people and turning against the decision of his own council, Pushmataha will see that proper punishment is meted out to him, which is death. You have made your choice; you have elected to fight with the British. The Americans have been our friends and we shall stand by them. We will furnish you safe conduct to the boundaries of this nation as properly befits the dignity of your office. Farewell, Tecumseh. You will see Pushmataha no more until we meet on the fateful warpath.

For Further Research

Books

John Francis Bannon, ed., *The Spanish Conquistadors: Men or Devils?* New York: Holt, Rinehart and Winston, 1960.

Leonardo Boff and Virgil Elizondo, eds., *1492–1992: The Voice of the Victims.* London: SCM Press, 1990.

Robert Burnette, *The Tortured Americans.* Englewood Cliffs, NJ: Prentice-Hall, 1971.

Colin G. Calloway, *New Worlds for All: Indians, Europeans, and the Remaking of Early America.* Baltimore, MD: Johns Hopkins University Press, 1997.

Colin G. Calloway, *The World Turned Upside Down: Indian Voices from Early America.* Boston: St. Martin's Press, 1994.

J.E. Chamberlin, *The Harrowing of Eden: White Attitudes Toward Native Americans.* New York: Seabury Press, 1975.

Christopher Columbus, *The Log of Christopher Columbus.* Translated by Robert H. Fuson. Camden, ME: International Marine Publishing, 1987.

Alfred W. Crosby Jr., *The Columbian Exchange: Biological and Cultural Consequences of 1492.* Westport, CT: Greenwood Press, 1972.

Miles H. Davidson, *Columbus Then and Now: A Life Re-Examined.* Norman, OK: University of Oklahoma Press, 1997.

Jean Descola, *The Conquistadors.* Translated by Malcolm Barnes. New York: Viking, 1957.

Bernal Díaz del Castillo, *The Conquest of New Spain.* Translated by J.M. Cohen. New York: Penguin, 1963.

Anthony Disney, ed., *Columbus and the Consequences of 1492.* Melbourne: La Trobe University Press, 1994.

Michael Dorris and Louis Erdrich, *The Crown of Columbus.* New York: HarperCollins, 1991.

John Dyson, *Columbus: For Gold, God, and Glory.* New York: Simon & Schuster, 1991.

Patricia de Fuentes, ed., *The Conquistadors: First-Person Accounts of the Conquest of Mexico.* New York: Orion Press, 1963.

John Hemming, *The Conquest of the Incas.* San Diego: Harcourt Brace Jovanovich, 1970.

Peter Charles Hoffer, ed., *Indians and Europeans: Selected Articles on Indian-White Relations in Colonial North America.* New York: Garland Publishing, 1988.

Washington Irving, *A History of the Life and Voyages of Christopher Columbus.* New York: G & C Carvill, 1828.

Hans Konig, *Columbus: His Enterprise, Exploding the Myth.* New York: Monthly Review Press, 1991.

Bartolomé de las Casas, *The Devastation of the Indies: A Brief Account.* Translated by Herma Briffault. New York: Seabury Press, 1974.

———, *In Defense of the Indians.* Translated by Stafford Poole. DeKalb, IL: Northern Illinois Univ. Press, 1974.

Miguel Leon-Portilla, *Pre-Columbian Literatures of Mexico.* Norman: Univ. of Oklahoma Press, 1969.

Miguel Leon-Portilla, ed., *The Broken Spears: The Aztec Account of the Conquest of Mexico.* Boston: Beacon Press, 1962.

R.H. Major, *Select Letters of Christopher Columbus, with Other Original Documents Relating to His First Four Voyages to the New World.* London: The Hakluyt Society, 1847. Reprinted 1961.

Jon Ewbank Manchip, *Cortes and the Downfall of the Aztec Empire.* New York: Carroll and Graf Publishers, 1996.

Samuel Eliot Morison, *Christopher Columbus, Mariner.* Boston: Little, Brown, 1955.

Toribio Motolinia, *Motolinia's History of the Indians of New Spain.* Translated and edited by Elizabeth Andros Foster. Westport, CT: Greenwood Press, 1973.

Alvar Nunez Cabeza de Vaca, *Relation of Nunez Cabeza de Vaca.* Ann Arbor, MI: University Microfilms, 1966.

Theodore Roosevelt, *The Winning of the West,* Vol. I. New York: G.P. Putnam's Sons, Knickerbocker Press, 1903.

Annette Rosenstiel, ed., *Red and White: Indian Views of the White Man. 1492–1982.* New York: Universe Books, 1983.

Stephen Summerhill, *Sinking Columbus: Contested History, Cultural Politics, and Mythmaking During the Quincentury.* Gainesville, FL: University Press of Florida, 2000.

Paolo Emilio Taviani, *Columbus: The Great Adventure.* Translated by Luciano F. Farina and Marc A. Beckwith. New York: Orion Books, 1991.

S. Lyman Tyler, ed., *Two Worlds: The Indian Encounters with the Europeans 1492–1509.* Salt Lake City: Univ. of Utah

Press, 1988.
W.C. Vanderweth, *Indian Oratory: Famous Speeches by Noted Indian Chieftains.* Norman: Univ. of Oklahoma Press, 1971.

Periodicals

Bill Bigelow, "Two Myths Are Not Better than One," *Monthly Review*, July/August 1992.

Rae Corelli, "To Celebrate or Repent? Critics Assail the Columbus Myth," *Maclean's*, August 5, 1991.

Michael Dorris, "Native Savages? We'll Drink to That," *The New York Times*, April 21, 1992.

Mark Falcoff, "Was 1492 a Mistake? Did Columbus Go Too Far?" *The American Enterprise*, January/February 1992.

Stephen Goode, "Debunking Columbus," *Insight*, October 21, 1991.

Suzan Shown Harjo, "We Have No Reason to Celebrate an Invasion," an interview with Barbara Miner. *Rethinking Schools*, October/November 1991.

Charles Krauthammer, "Hail Columbus, Dead White Male," *Time*, May 27, 1991.

James R. McGraw, "God Is Also Red: An Interview with Vine Deloria Jr.," *Christianity and Crisis*, September 15, 1975.

James Muldoon, "The Columbus Quincentennial: Should Christians Celebrate It?" *America*, October 27, 1990.

Charles W. Polzer, "Reflections on the Quincentenary," *America*, November 16, 1991.

Ernesto Sabato, "The 'Nina,' the 'Pinta,' and the Debate They Started: A Latin American Writer Defends Christopher Columbus," *World Press Review*, October 1991.

Robert Allen Warrior, "Columbus Quincentennial Is Nothing to Celebrate," *Utne Reader*, November/December 1991.

Samuel M. Wilson, "Columbus, My Enemy," *Natural History*, December 1990.

Index

140